GOD Loves YOU

AND THERE'S NOTHING ANYONE CAN DO ABOUT IT

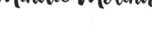

Mindie Molina

WESTBOW
PRESS®

A DIVISION OF THOMAS NELSON
& ZONDERVAN

Scripture taken from the King James Version of the Bible.

WestBow Press books may be ordered through booksellers or by contacting:

WestBow Press
A Division of Thomas Nelson & Zondervan
1663 Liberty Drive
Bloomington, IN 47403
www.westbowpress.com
1 (866) 928-1240

ISBN: 978-1-9736-0955-1 (sc)
ISBN: 978-1-9736-0957-5 (hc)
ISBN: 978-1-9736-0956-8 (e)

Library of Congress Control Number: 2017918060

Print information available on the last page.

WestBow Press rev. date: 3/27/2018

CONTENTS

PREFACE

The Spirit of the Lord GOD is upon me; because the LORD hath anointed me to preach good tidings unto the meek; he hath sent me to bind up the brokenhearted, to proclaim liberty to the captives, and the opening of the prison to them that are bound.
—Isaiah 61:1

When Jesus first began his public ministry, he went into his hometown synagogue, pulled out the above passage in Isaiah, and read it aloud. These words set the tone for what was to become of him and his life—to preach good tidings to the meek, bind up the brokenhearted, and proclaim liberty and freedom.

My husband shared this verse with me, and I couldn't help feeling like this is why I wrote this book. I wrote it so that all people who have resentment for God because of things that have been said or done to them can find peace and love in knowing that God loves them. So that those who have been misled about Jesus and Christianity because of someone else's behavior, actions, or words can decide for themselves who Jesus is and what it means to be a Christian.

Most important, I want whoever reads this book to learn about the love God has for all of us. In every chapter you will find proof in multiple scriptures that God loves you. No matter what your relationship with God is or has been, find out what the Bible says about your relationship with him. God wants you to let go of the stereotypes given to Christians. Let go of the things you've been told in the past and read the truth about Jesus and how much God loves you.

Reading this book may be difficult at times. You may want to throw it against the wall (which is what one editor told me—that people would throw this book against the wall), but I beg you to push on. If you start feeling frustrated, then you are more than likely the type of person for whom I have written this, which is *exactly* why you should keep reading it. Once you have finished the book, then go ahead and give it a throw if you feel like it.

You should know that I am just a normal person—mother, wife, daughter, sister, friend, and not really equipped to write a book. Then again, is anyone truly just and qualified to write a book about God Almighty? I think not. The Bible is the only book that is just. If you are looking for credibility in an author, I'd stick with the Bible. I have no formal education in biblical studies, but I can tell you that studying the Bible never ends. You don't get a certificate that says you have mastered the Word of God. The Bible is complex yet so simple. There are layers and layers of knowledge and discoveries in that one book, and I believe that no one can uncover them all in a lifetime. It is the ultimate Book.

This book is of no comparison. It is compiled of random thoughts and messages that have been on my heart, coupled with some scriptures that I think are crucial for us to understand. We must know what Jesus was teaching us along with how we ought to be as Christians. If I had to sum it up with one verse, it would be this one:

"Nay, in all these things we are more than conquerors through him that loved us. For I am persuaded, that neither death, nor life, nor angels, nor principalities, nor powers, nor things present, nor things to come, Nor height, nor depth, nor any other creature, shall be able to separate us from the love of God, which is in Christ Jesus our Lord" (Romans 8:37–39).

Whether you were raised in a church, pastored a church, or don't believe in God, you can benefit from this book. Whether or not you believe Jesus was the son of God, you should read this book to learn how to coexist with people who do believe. My hope is that there will be a dismantling of the hatred and battles over how someone should live and what is acceptable and what's not. This book will teach you how Christians should treat you; if they believe in Jesus, then they should represent his teachings.

Sometimes nonbelievers don't want to be around "religious people" because of the many misconceptions about what religious people are like. I want this book to help you have a better understanding. Most important, I want you to be able to defend yourself (in a peaceful and educated way) against a Christian who isn't treating you right. Beyond that, perhaps you will become more comfortable with this Jesus guy.

As a Christian, it's easy to be swayed away from the scriptures and the original messages that Jesus taught us. This book is a good reminder of our purpose here on earth. At a time in the world when we are divided, it is so important for the Christians of the world to be reminded of what God expects of us. It is a crucial time for us to be on our best behaviors, as the world is watching. We must remember who we represent and we *must* represent him to the best of our abilities.

It is my hope that this book will be an awakening to all Christians—an awakening and a reminder that Jesus and his way is the right way—the only way.

I wrote this book because I felt that God wanted me to write it. For a year, I had an overwhelming conviction that I was not doing what God was asking me to do if I wasn't writing. My goal was to write ten short books, which later became the chapters of this book. It was that conviction that held me accountable and got it done. The conviction was stronger than anything I have ever experienced. I felt very sad and guilty any time I ignored this request. The first time I started typing, I was like a kid forced to clean her room— pouty and irritated—but I carried on. It has taken much longer than I imagined it would, but through this process I have come to realize many things about who I am and why things happen or don't happen. Unexplainable things occurred throughout the first year of my writing; for instance, I wrote three books that mysteriously were lost on my computer. One was deleted right before my eyes. It was heartbreaking and discouraging to see my work robbed from me.

I am the mom of a toddler, I run a business, and I am a slave to my hobbies and home. By the time I finished the draft of this book, I was eight months pregnant with my second child. I like to work hard and play hard, and writing books doesn't fit in anywhere. Therefore, knowing that the time I had set aside was also robbed from me was frustrating. In the end, I used those misfortunes as a sign and a motivation that this *is* what God wants me to do, and it *is not* what the devil wants me to do. Those three books were powerful, and two were my favorites, so why wouldn't the devil do what he could to get rid of them? I took that as a compliment and started over, refusing to be set back or kept from my calling.

I am excited to share with you some of the things God has put on my heart. I have no clue why or how it may make a difference. I am just thrilled to have followed through with his request, and I sleep in peace, knowing I did it.

There were nights when I would lie awake, crying, because I felt that God was ignoring my requests. His reply was, "You are ignoring *my* requests. Write these books." Knowing that I have no credentials or right to be guiding others in their relationships with God, it was hard for me. I kept saying it was stupid, and I didn't want to do it. At some point, I decided that was not why I would write; I would write for no other purpose than to fulfill God's request of me. What happens now is not my problem. I did my part.

Writing a book usually starts with a purpose—what is the point of the book? Then an outline is developed, along with highlighting the important messages of the book. I had none of that. I frequently asked God, "What is the point of this?" I really didn't get it. It seemed a little silly, and I was going at it blind, but in faith I pressed on. I would have random experiences, or a message would come into my heart that would inspire the next chapter. Before I knew it, I had my ten.

It wasn't until several months after finishing the ten short books (now chapters) that God revealed to me the bottom line—the ultimate message he wanted me to share with you. This moment, for me, was the greatest part of this experience because *finally* all of my work made sense, and it now was something dear to my heart and something in which I saw value.

As you read, if you take nothing else from this book, take this:

God loves you. And there's nothing
anyone can do about it.

1 CHRISTIAN CONFUSION

As a young girl, I wanted to be saved. I wanted to seek God and live a godly life because I loved God and wanted to serve him. I wanted to submit my life to him, repent, and live righteously—all the things the preacher said on Sundays. I wanted to do that, but I was really confused about how to do it and concerned about my ability to do it. I was certain I would fail. Despite my innocence, I knew righteousness and always doing what's right was not realistic. Then one night—September 18, 1997, to be exact—I was driving home under a beautiful starlit sky. As I drove along a gravel road through dark woods, I replayed what I had read at a Bible study I'd attended with my brother. My brother had been seeking God but, at first, hadn't found the answers for which he was searching. Once he found them, he had an overwhelming desire to share the information with the world. He was very excited and happy and wanted his little sister to share that same joy.

That night in my car, the truth was revealed to me. The hope and freedom I had been searching for was finally here. The understanding and certainty I had wanted relieved me of any doubt or fear I'd had. A light bulb went off inside my head, and I never felt burdened ever again.

I have had peace in my heart and soul for eighteen years. I finally overcame my confusion about being saved. The devil implants doubt and confusion into our world to keep us, perhaps, from ever experiencing that hope and freedom that Jesus offers us.

As people who seek to be Christians or religious people, we have a common thread: we *fear*. We fear going to hell. We fear being punished by God while we're alive. We have those same fears for our families and friends. So how do we avoid that fear? We avoid sin, and we beg our friends and family to avoid sin. We may freak out about it because we are afraid—for ourselves and for our loved ones.

"He that believeth on the Son hath everlasting life: and he that believeth not the Son shall not see life; but the wrath of God abideth on him" (John 3:36).

For me, that fear is gone. It left eighteen years ago. I want that fear to leave *all* the people of the world because that fear causes confusion and division among us all. It causes Christians to misrepresent what being a Christian is. Let's look at that confusion.

CONFUSION NO. 1

A Christian cannot sin.

Growing up in the church, I heard things like, "Repent and turn from your wicked ways. Turn from your sin." I would hear Christians talk about sinners and their sins—thieves, liars, murderers, and much more. I tried to follow the Ten Commandments, but that seemed impossible for me. Was I really honoring my mother and father? Had I really never told a lie, not even fibbed a tiny bit? Had I never taken something that didn't belong to me? Sure, I'd never killed anyone, but that was just one commandment of the ten.

Am I going to hell? What if I do something without knowing it's a sin?

I believe in God. I believe in Jesus. I just don't believe in myself enough to know that if I repent that I won't end up doing something stupid again tomorrow. Or even in the next twenty minutes.

Why are Christians called hypocrites? Self-righteous? Judgmental? Does the general public hold an expectation that if a person claims to be a Christian, then that person will not sin? Must a Christian live righteously and be perfect, making only the best choices and doing only good things? Why is it when a Christian says or does something bad, people say, "Oh, I thought you were a Christian"?

None of that makes sense, even though I see and hear it all the time. It's like there's a wall between being a Christian and a non-Christian. Why would anyone want to be a judgmental hypocrite? For me, this perception is heartbreaking and needs to end. The way I feel about it this: Jesus Christ hung on a cross, was beaten, died, and went to hell, all in the name of our forgiveness. So is it true that if you are a Christian, you will not or cannot sin? No. One world, one people, one problem—we *all* fall short. We all sin. We all need forgiveness.

God cursed the earth when Adam and Eve ate the forbidden fruit, so there is no escaping it. Anyone who portrays that he or she is *not* living in sin or is *not* a sinner is lying, and that's a sin. To be a Christian just means you are forgiven for your sins, not that you don't or won't sin. You will sin again and again, Christian or not. The hope and freedom is in knowing that you are going to heaven when you die, regardless of your sin.

Many people live with the burden of feeling scared to sin or scared they will forget to repent for their sins. Will you go to hell? No, Jesus died for your sins—all of them. You are set free of the burden, the guilt, and the punishment. You are forgiven—forever.

> Even the righteousness of God *which is* by faith of Jesus Christ unto all and upon all them that believe: for there is no difference: For all have sinned, and come short of the glory of God; Being justified freely by his grace through the redemption that is in Christ Jesus: Whom God hath set forth *to be* a propitiation through faith in his blood, to declare his righteousness for the remission of sins that are past, through the forbearance of God; To declare, *I say*, at this time his righteousness: that he might be just, and the justifier of him which believeth in Jesus. (Romans 3:22–26)

Whether or not you believe in Jesus or God or anything, please do not project to the world that Christians *cannot* sin. It isn't true, and it is robbing Jesus Christ of his glory, for he came to this earth, suffered, and died for all the sins of the world. Being a Christian means giving Jesus that glory and being grateful for his doing, not claiming that you do no wrong.

It also is not fair for nonbelievers to think that Christians do not sin because if that is true, what hope do nonbelievers have? Are they supposed to believe in themselves enough to become a Christian? Should they believe they have the ability to fight off sin all on their own, so that they can be righteous? No. That's a lie. They cannot and will not ever accomplish this, nor will anyone. Hope and freedom is in the death of Jesus Christ. He died for all the sins of the world.

"For God so loved the world, that he gave his only begotten Son, that whosoever believeth in him should not perish, but have everlasting life. For God sent not his Son into the world to condemn the world; but that the world through him might be saved. He that believeth on him is not condemned: but he that believeth not is condemned already, because he hath not believed in the name of the only begotten Son of God" (John 3:16–18).

CONFUSION NO. 2

You must repent or ask for forgiveness every time you sin. If you don't, and then you die, you'll go to hell.

If you want to get Christians fired up, just get a bunch of them together and ask about this one. There is such a division over whether or not you have to ask for forgiveness *every time* you sin. I say no; you are forgiven forever. Forever sealed in the book of life. God accepted you the moment you accepted Jesus Christ as a real-life person who was the Son of God; who currently sits in heaven next to God; who was hung on a cross, beaten, stabbed in the side with a sword, and crucified; who went to hell; and who rose from the dead—all so that you and I and the rest of the world could be forgiven of our sins.

If you believe this to be true, then why would you ever need to do anything? Wasn't what Jesus did enough? Don't you feel guilty all of the time? Don't you want to get on your knees and say thank you, over and over again? Don't you feel condemned when you sin, when you go against what you know is best but you give in and fail? Don't you think God had all of that in mind as he watched his Son being beaten and stabbed, nails driven threw his hands, and left to die, sacrificed like an animal? It makes me feel bad. I want to meet Jesus when I die and say, "Thank you. I was a goner. I had no strength, no hope, and no freedom without you and what you did for me."

Yes, there are many times when I say, "I am sorry, Jesus. I am sorry for how I have acted, and I will try to do better for my own sake." We know that bad leads to bad. I don't want bad or trouble for myself. I want to live a fun and happy life without drama. However, I see no need to keep score of my sins and ask for repentance over and over to a God who has already done enough to pay for my sins, over and over and over again. I could never do enough bad to outweigh God's only Son dying—and not just dying but being tortured and humiliated. His death was brutal.

Grace means to give something without expecting something in return. You may know the song "Amazing Grace." Why is it so popular? Because God's grace is amazing! God gave us grace with Jesus and his sacrifice. He doesn't expect anything in return. He just wants us to believe, which means to have faith—to believe and have faith and die with confidence that we are forgiven; to live a life free of the burden of guilt and fear. The devil can keep us separated from God and his offer by keeping us afraid, feeling guilty, and incapable of living up to some sort of "Christian standards." *There are no standards.* Believe it or not, Jesus came to save the world. Think about that: *Jesus came to save the world.* Can it be any clearer or simpler? He came to save the world, not to condemn it. The truth is that God loves *all of us.*

They say unto him, Master, this woman was taken in adultery, in the very act. Now Moses in the law commanded us, that such should be stoned: but what sayest thou? This they said, tempting him, that they might have to accuse him. But Jesus stooped down, and with *his* finger wrote on the ground, *as though he heard them not*. So when they continued asking him, he lifted up himself, and said unto them, He that is without sin among you, let him first cast a stone at her. And again he stooped down, and wrote on the ground. And they which heard *it*, being convicted by *their own* conscience, went out one by one, beginning at the eldest, *even* unto the last: and Jesus was left alone, and the woman standing in the midst. When Jesus had lifted up himself, and saw none but the woman, he said unto her, Woman, where are those thine accusers? Hath no man condemned thee? She said, No man, Lord. And Jesus said unto her, neither do I condemn thee: go, and sin no more. (John 8:4–11)

I love this story. Jesus said, "Neither do I condemn thee." In my dumbest moments and my darkest days, GOD never turned from me. He stayed with me in the dark. Though I failed myself, I did not fail my Lord. He loves me. He knows my heart. He knows my actions. He knows my regrets and my burdens, and he loves me. He knows my story. He knows my sins. He knows every detail and every reason I ended up choosing the path I chose. He was there and witnessed it all and knew my heart, and he loves me. Am I perfect? Of course not. I thank Jesus Christ for dying for my sins. Who on this earth can judge me or you? They may cast their stones now, but they won't cast them before God.

God knows; people don't. God loves you! Jesus died for your sins of the past, present, and future. He wants the glory. Give it to him. Praise him. Thank him. Don't insult him with all of your calculated recollections of your wrongdoings. Do not put on an act of repentance, for you have been forgiven only through the actions of Jesus Christ.

Instead, rejoice and live a life of freedom and peace. Wake up confident. Die confident. Give God the credit that you are saved forever. Never look back. Never doubt again. Be so free that you are like a bird in the sky, whistling the most beautiful song. Let the world see you soaring and ask you, "Why are you so happy and free?" And you can say, "Jesus died for me. I am free!"

The following verse says God is the beginning and the ending. Let's not kid ourselves. God knows every move we ever will make in our lifetimes here on this earth. If he is going to offer forgiveness to us, it won't be temporary. It will be for eternity. He knows what lies ahead, and from what I have read, he took that into account when he sent Jesus to die on the cross. Again, it wasn't just for today; it was for eternity.

"I am Alpha and Omega, the beginning and the ending, saith the Lord, which is, and which was, and which is to come, the Almighty" (Revelation 1:8).

CONFUSION NO. 3

You must be washed in the blood of the Lamb.

"And the blood of Jesus Christ his Son cleanseth us from all sin. If we say that we have no sin, we deceive ourselves, and the truth is not in us. If we confess our sins, he is faithful and just to forgive us *our* sins, and to cleanse us from all unrighteousness. If we say that we have not sinned, we make him a liar, and his word is not in us" (John 8:7–30).

Who wants to be washed in the blood of anything? Well, the above scripture refers to the blood of Jesus Christ. On the cross, the soldier pierced Jesus's side, and he bled. That blood was an atonement for our sins—a sacrificial necessity, I guess. You can read more about it in the Bible, but my point is that when you believe in Jesus and his sacrifice for your sins, when you believe that Jesus did it to pay the debt of your sins, a spiritual intervention happens to you.

Your sins don't go away, but they get washed over with the blood of Jesus, and you appear perfect—bright and new. You no longer walk in darkness. You are free of the sins of the world—the darkness. That blood on you makes you glow everywhere you go. Again, you still have sin, but because you are washed in the blood of the Lamb, you have Jesus's blood on you, covering those sins. Whether they are today's sins, yesterday's sins, or next year's sins, you're covered. Just be thankful and know that you are forgiven. Give glory. Praise him.

The following verse somehow brought it all together for me eighteen years ago. I came to this realization that all this "saved" business and being a Christian was about being set free from the laws of this world and living for the spiritual world. Seems kind of crazy, but read this passage over and over until you get it. The spirit of Jesus Christ is in us and with us always. We are with him already; we have been protected from our sins and made spiritually perfect. Meanwhile, this body (flesh) and this life are doomed to failure. In the flesh (here on earth), we are not able to live up to God's standards (the biblical laws from before Christ). Therefore, we have to cling to the spirit of Jesus Christ and look beyond this world, this life, and these failures. They will die off, but we will live eternally with Jesus Christ.

> There is therefore now no condemnation to them which are in Christ Jesus, who walk not after the flesh, but after the Spirit. For the law of the Spirit of life in Christ Jesus hath made me free from the law of sin and death. For what the law could not do, in that it was weak through the flesh, God sending his own Son in the likeness of sinful flesh, and for sin, condemned sin in the flesh: That the righteousness of the law might be fulfilled in us, who walk not after the flesh, but after the Spirit. For they that are after the flesh do mind the things of the flesh; but they

that are after the Spirit the things of the Spirit. For to be carnally minded *is* death; but to be spiritually minded *is* life and peace. Because the carnal mind *is* enmity against God: for it is not subject to the law of God, neither indeed can be. So then they that are in the flesh cannot please God. (Romans 8:1–8)

Being a Christian, to me, means living in the spirit world. It doesn't mean I don't sin. It doesn't mean I am righteous. It means this real-world life is already dead to me. What happens here doesn't matter. I'm already in the spiritual world with my heavenly Father and his Son, Jesus Christ. I want the same for all my friends and family. I'll even say that I want it for the entire world—the same world Jesus came to save. There is no race, gender, ethnicity, or social class. There is no comparisons of sin or wondering if something is or isn't a sin. There is no question of which is the appropriate lifestyle. What works for you may not work for others. We all have our own ways to get through life, and the *only* one who knows what lies in our hearts and the reasons behind what we do is God Almighty.

Before you say what should or shouldn't be, realize that *you don't know.* Worry about what you *do* know—your life and your relationship with a God who loves you and wants you to love also.

In my world, I am me. I am unworthy. My body is a sinner, but my spirit is set free. I am flying like a bird. There is no darkness. There is only light. I am at peace and live life knowing I am one with God. I am free. I am happy. Final destination—heaven.

I HOLD THE POWER

Though the spirit-world stuff is amazing, and I try to keep my eye on eternity, life on earth is still very challenging. Like all people, I have my battles. Whether it's in my career, my family, my relationships, or my own weaknesses, I have my moments. But those moments are always resolved when I rely on God to handle them.

I'll never forget the first time I surrendered an argument over to God. It appeared there was no winning this particular conflict, and I was ready to give up. I was exhausted from the drama and confrontation. I just wanted it to end. Somehow, I decided that my only hope was in God. I prayed for God to take control and, more than anything, I prayed that he would make the argument end. Within seconds of my giving up the fight and handing it over to God, God ended it. Just like that. It happened so fast in response to my prayer that it actually freaked me out. The person with whom I was arguing had a sudden physical issue that resulted in the person no longer having any interest in the discussion. I was a little shocked and dumbfounded. Only God can pull off something like that.

I couldn't stop thinking about that experience. Would God give someone a physical problem in order to protect me and answer my prayer? Though it was a minor physical issue, it was an immediate answer to my prayer. How God decides to handle a situation or put an end to evil is up to him, but this experience lifted me up and empowered me. It proved to me without a shadow of a doubt that God loves me *and* that he does have my back and wants to protect me. Had I known how quickly and easily God would end the conversation and allow me to have peace, I would have prayed to him and given up long before I did.

This particular experience made me realize that God has more power and more capabilities than I have, and he knows more than I know and can accomplish so much more than I can. On a large scale or small scale, God can put an end to anything.

"For we wrestle not against flesh and blood, but against principalities, against powers, against the rulers of the darkness of this world, against spiritual wickedness in high places" (Ephesians 6:12).

We have to remember that the bad things that happen in our lives are not because of the people in our lives. Bad things happen because of the principalities, powers, and rulers of the darkness. The people in our lives are just people affected by those principalities, powers, and rulers of the darkness. We only need to turn it over to God.

"And what [is] the exceeding greatness of his power to us-ward who believe, according to the working of his mighty power, Which he wrought in Christ, when he raised him from the dead, and set [him] at his own right hand in the heavenly [places], Far above all principality, and power, and might, and dominion, and every name that is named, not only in this world, but also in that which is to come" (Ephesians 1:19–21).

I began to think about other situations in my life where I wished I had prayed to God to fix things or make things end. Maybe you are dealing with something that is damaging you or with someone who is hurting you. I suggest giving it over to a God who loves you and has your back. Let him step in and take over. You may be surprised by the outcome.

I have since begun turning things over to God. Big or small, I have let go of fighting for my happiness and peace. I have put that burden on God. He can overcome battles I can't see or may not know exist. Why not put your faith in him? Why not let him deal with the people in your life who cause you grief—remember that it's not them but the evil that needs to be destroyed. That is the power you hold, after all. If you want to hold the power, you have to give it to God.

Imagine you are the promoter of the greatest boxer who ever lived—the strongest, the wisest, the undefeated champion. Another boxer has just challenged your boxer to a fight. Will you step into the ring and fight the other boxer yourself? Of course not. You will stand in the corner, cheering on and praising your boxer as he defeats the enemy.

That's God. He is your champion, here to fight for you. Let him do the fighting. Let him put evil to rest. Let him put an end to whatever is hurting you. The greatest part is that he can do it peacefully, lovingly, and quietly. You focus on living peacefully and putting your faith in God, that he will overcome anyone who tries to rob you of that peace. It's his way in his time. I don't want to portray God as a violent force, but he is *God*, and he is to be feared and respected. I'm pretty sure he has the power to do whatever he sees fit. I know with certainty that he loves you and will defeat evil for you.

"The LORD shall fight for you, and ye shall hold your peace" (Exodus 14:14).

On the flip side, perhaps you should consider what could be in store for you if you are the instigator of problems. What if the person you are destroying with your words or actions is surrendering it to God, praying for God to make *you* stop? I don't want to be in the crossfire of God's fury at any time, not ever. I'd like to be on the good side of God at all times. The last thing I need is to be bedridden with the flu, or break out in hives, or have the worst toothache ever, all so I can't cause harm. Please don't let me be the one in the ring with God!

I also have realized that I don't need to be afraid. "What shall we then say to these things? If God be for us, who can be against us?" (Romans 8:31).

Do you believe that? How strong is your faith? Since I witnessed God's taking action in my life, my faith is pretty strong.

I had an experience in my business life, where a potential client turned potentially dangerous. I'm not accustomed to people threatening me, so I was a little freaked out. Even though I believed he was just a bully, trying to push me around through fear, I still was concerned. Then I remembered the power of my God. I said to myself, *If this guy drops dead from a heart attack, or he catches a rare disease, I'll know that he* did *have bad intentions and that God took care of it for me.* It may sound like a joke, but don't ever underestimate the power of God and his love for us.

If Satan thinks for one second that God isn't looking out for us, he's got another thing coming. I hold the power of God. It is in me. It follows me. I have surrendered to it. And it is a mighty power that those people with bad intentions shouldn't mess with. There is nothing that can protect them. There is nowhere they can run or hide. My God will find them, and he will protect me. He has my back—and yours too.

"Yea, though I walk through the valley of the shadow of death, I will fear no evil: for thou art with me; thy rod and thy staff they comfort me" (Psalm 23:4).

"Let us therefore come boldly unto the throne of grace, that we may obtain mercy, and find grace to help in time of need" (Hebrews 4:16).

"O God, be not far from me: O my God, make haste for my help" (Psalm 71:12).

Does this mean I'm arrogant and have no respect for people? Does it mean I do and say whatever I want? No. Again, I don't want to be the one God has to stop.

It does mean, however, that I am not going to be bullied, or put down, or impacted by what others say. My response will be in prayer. I will pray and ask God to deal with the situation. I will pray for the safety of my family and me. I will pray for peace and joy. I don't want drama. I don't want violence, not for me or my family.

I have my flare-ups of anger, and I rant and rave at times, but my faith tells me that God can handle it. I have no idea how, but I know that he will. I know that if I just keep quiet and rely on him that he will take care of it for me. I know because of his love, his grace, and his mercy. All I can do is be thankful.

The following verse is a reminder that his gifts to us (including his protection) will never be matched by anything we could possibly do for him. At some point, we have to accept that and be grateful.

> I love the LORD, because he hath heard my voice and my supplications. Because he hath inclined his ear unto me, therefore will I call upon him as long as I live. The sorrows of death compassed me, and the pains of hell gat hold upon me: I found trouble and sorrow. Then called I upon the name of the LORD; O LORD, I beseech thee, deliver my soul. Gracious is the LORD, and righteous; yea, our God is merciful.
>
> The LORD preserveth the simple: I was brought low, and he helped me. Return unto thy rest, O my soul; for the LORD hath dealt bountifully with thee. For thou hast delivered my soul from death, mine eyes from tears, and my feet from falling. I will walk before the LORD in the land of the living. I believed, therefore have I spoken: I was greatly afflicted: I said in my haste, All men are liars. What shall I render unto the LORD for all his benefits toward me? (Psalm 1–11)

The power of God is immeasurable. It cannot be harnessed. It cannot be controlled. It cannot be predicted. It cannot be outdone. All you can do is submit to it, stay on the good side of it, know that God loves you, accept it, and be thankful.

In a world where it sometimes feels like people are out to get you and in a life where not everyone is on your side, rely on God to handle your battles. Accept his power as your own, and let it work for you. God loves you, and there's nothing anyone can do about it.

GOAL-DRIVEN 3

I married my high school sweetheart and set out on the road to happiness. We bought a house and a couple of cars, went to college, and worked full time. We followed the recipe for happiness. It seemed that everything would fall into place as long as we did our part. I never understood how people could get their lives so messed up. God gave us such a simple recipe for a blessed life. What was the problem?

I always thought that people needed to just tighten up, walk the line, do what God said, and live right. Then everything would just fall into place. I was Little Miss Clueless, looking at the world as if the only reason I had never been faced with adversity was because of me and all my doings. My life was smooth and easy because I did the "right" things.

There is a problem, however, with that way of thinking. The one who deserves the glory is God, not us. The reason things were good for me was because God allowed them to be good. And I know that when my fairy tale ended in divorce, my strife, my "black-out period," as I like to call it, was because God allowed those things to happen. He had to do so. It was the only way to get me to stop giving myself all the credit. Once my life went downhill a couple of times while I was doing everything I could to keep that from happening, I realized that I didn't have any control after all and that all my *doing* was pointless, meaningless, powerless, and simply worthless. I was worthless. Counting on myself to make everything right was worthless.

It was then that I started looking at the world from a different perspective. It was the first time I had ever looked at people without judgment. I never realized I was judging them until I looked at them *without* judging them. I became empathetic and understanding. I finally knew that they had no control. They didn't do anything to deserve what they were going through. I had to be put through the fire myself to realize this, but I did finally get it.

Those times that I struggled, failed, messed up, and acted like a moron were the times that taught me the most. It was when my life hit bottom that I turned to God. It was then that I relied on him. It was then that I discovered who I am and—more importantly—who I am not.

As a girl, I believed my successes and achievements would define me. Looking back, I realize my failures and defeats have made me who I am. Thank God for those times because without them, the person I would have become would not be the person I would want to be.

"And we know that all things work together for good to them that love God, to them who are the called according to [his] purpose" (Romans 8:28).

Now I live my life for God and through God, with all things relying on God. Whether things are good or bad, up or down, I know God has his hand in it. I know I am not alone and that I don't have to beat myself up or despise others for the things they do. Maybe God is using the situation to teach me and guide me. The one thing I know is that he loves me, and everything is going to be okay.

"Casting all your care upon him; for he careth for you" (1 Peter 5:7).

Those are beautiful words—"for he careth for you." It's good to know when you are going through hard times. It's hard to believe and trust sometimes, but if you do, it will help. I promise.

Sometimes things are awesome but we are *not* so awesome. Sometimes we take the blessing for granted. We rely on ourselves more than we rely on God. We start to possess things and take credit for things that God is doing. We feel more entitled than grateful. I've learned this lesson the hard way, and since then, I have been able to recognize when others also are learning the hard way. When things are awesome, I now know God is blessing me. I now know to take it as a gift or sometimes as a loan. Awesome doesn't last forever. Enjoy it while it lasts, and keep your grip loose because the tighter you cling to those blessings, the worse it will hurt when they are gone.

You know the verse—"The Lord giveth and the Lord taketh away." That is so true. He will give because he loves you, but if you cling to your blessings more than to him, you'll be on your own. And isn't that the message you've sent God? I'm on my own. I did it. I got it on my own, so I am on my own. It's better, however, to *never* be on your own. It's better to keep God around and to keep him involved and in charge. He is capable of so much more than we are. What he can do for us is so much better than what we can do for ourselves.

"In all thy ways acknowledge him, and he shall direct thy paths" (Proverbs 3:6).

God loves us and wants the glory to go to him. When we live as if we are in control of everything, or when everything is out of control, and we are trying desperately to figure it out, that's when we should be clinging to God and putting faith in him to bring things under control for us. And when things are under control, we should give him glory for it. That's the real deal. When we find ourselves relying on God to do everything, we are in a real-deal relationship with God.

I love setting goals. In my adult life, I always have been in business, and in the corporate world it's all about goals. I am competitive, and when I have a goal, it's like a race to the finish line. When I surpass that goal, I feel like a champion—and I like that. I like feeling like a superstar. I like for other people to ask me how I did it. I like to talk about it as if it was easy. But the truth is that I would sacrifice everything to reach that goal and do whatever it takes.

Setting goals and making resolutions is all about me. There's no glory for God. There's no room for him when I do all the work to accomplish my goals or when I make the sacrifices. It's really just about me. I did it for years. Year after year, I would make my list of ten personal goals, and year after year, I would cross out the stuff I accomplished and carry over the rest for the next year.

When I look back, I can see how my life progressed and how I grew through those lists. I can also look back and see the areas of my life that were neglected, and it makes me sad to see that some of my dreams did not come true. I can see the things that didn't take precedence—things that really mattered to me. Taking guitar lessons is one example. It may not seem like a big deal, but this has been on my list for over a decade. At what point will I cross it off? Having a list of goals doesn't always bring that feeling of being a champion. Sometimes I get the feeling of being a failure.

One night, during a dark, lonely part of my life, I lay in bed, feeling like a failure. I felt I had no hope or worth. No matter what I did, it didn't seem to be enough. I never have been one to ask God for things. After all, I was born into the United States of America. Isn't that enough? *Why should God help me*, I thought, *when there are people starving around the world? Kids are being abused, wars are being fought, and people are dying. I think his time would be better spent tending to those people. I am fine. I will pull through this. I will figure it out. I'm healthy, I'm smart, and I have no excuse.*

Then I read the following scripture, and it spoke to me. I had read it before, but this time, for whatever reason, it really was driven into my heart. It was as if God wanted me to understand what he was saying and really accept it.

> And I say unto you, Ask, and it shall be given you; seek, and ye shall find; knock, and it shall be opened unto you. For every one that asketh receiveth; and he that seeketh findeth; and to him that knocketh it shall be opened. If a son shall ask bread of any of you that is a father, will he give him a stone? Or if [he ask] a fish, will he for a fish give him a serpent? Or if he shall ask an egg, will he offer him a scorpion? If ye then, being evil, know how to give good gifts unto your children: how much more shall [your] heavenly Father give the Holy Spirit to them that ask him? (Luke 11:9–13)

Think about your son or daughter, your niece or nephew, and how much you love him or her. When you love someone, it brings you joy to see that person get the things he or she wants. Like that Christmas your son got the bicycle or the video game he wanted. Wasn't it fun buying it as a surprise and seeing the look on his face when he opened it?

It's actually a better feeling to see children receive the toys they have wanted than to buy yourself something. It doesn't matter if you're a parent; this is a feeling that anyone can easily understand—bringing a child that kind of joy. When you get to experience a child's surprise and delight, isn't that the greatest feeling? It's moments like that when people say, "This is what life is about."

> At the same time came the disciples unto Jesus, saying, Who is the greatest in the kingdom of heaven? And Jesus called a little child unto him, and set him in the midst of them, And said, Verily I say unto you, Except ye be converted, and become as little children, ye shall not enter into the kingdom of heaven. Whosoever therefore shall humble himself as this little child, the same is greatest in the kingdom of heaven. And whoso shall receive one such little child in my name receiveth me. (Matthew 18:1–5)

God is our Father. He wants us to humble ourselves. Rather than believe we are amazing grown-ups with talents, experiences, knowledge, and capabilities, he wants us to be like children. Arrogance and trying to prove something doesn't do anything for him. He is the ultimate arrogance, and he can prove all things, so who are we trying to impress anyway?

Just as we feel wonderful when giving a child a gift, God has the same experience when he gives us the things we want, when he surprises us with blessings or the things we've been praying for. This is what life's about for him too. It's not our being selfish and not deserving anything. It's not his needing to take care of all the other problems in the world. He is God! He can do it all. He is the richest, most powerful Dad in the world, and we are his kids. Isn't that great news? One of the greatest joys he has as a Father is giving us the things we want, the desires of our hearts.

Think about how sad it makes him if you never give him the chance to be a Dad to you. You never ask for anything, so he doesn't know what to give you. You get whatever you want on your own, so you never thank him or make him feel like he matters to you.

Imagine if you were a dad whose kids never accepted your gifts. They never asked for a bike or a new toy, and so they never said the words, "Look what my dad got me!"

It's a special part of being a parent, and it is a special part of being God.

After that night of my feeling as if I was failing at my goals, I realized what I needed to do—what God wanted me to do. I needed to turn my goal lists over to God. I needed to allow God the opportunity to truly bless me. It seemed silly at first, but some of the greatest moments in my journey as a believer came from this list. Seeing what God is capable of and seeing that he does love me is not silly. Really knowing what it's like to feel blessed is a greater feeling than anything I have ever achieved on my own.

So how do we go about being like a child with a Christmas list without feeling like an idiot or a selfish, spoiled brat? First, read the following verses, and then I will tell you.

"And whatever you ask in prayer, you will receive, if you have faith" (Matthew 21:22).

"Therefore I tell you, whatever you ask in prayer, believe that you have received it, and it will be yours" (Mark 11:24).

"Whatever you ask in my name, this I will do, that the Father may be glorified in the Son. If you ask me anything in my name, I will do it" (John 14:13–14).

"Do not be anxious about anything, but in everything by prayer and supplication with thanksgiving let your requests be made known to God. And the peace of God, which surpasses all understanding, will guard your hearts and your minds in Christ Jesus" (Philippians 4:6–7).

"Delight thyself also in the LORD; and he shall give thee the desires of thine heart (Psalm 37:4).

"Commit thy way unto the LORD; trust also in him; and he shall bring [it] to pass" (Psalm 37:5).

"But seek ye first the kingdom of God, and his righteousness; and all these things shall be added unto you" (Matthew 6:33).

"Trust in the LORD with all thine heart; and lean not unto thine own understanding" (Proverbs 3:5).

So let me recap:

1. Ask in prayer in the name of Jesus, and you will receive.
2. Have faith, so much that you believe it's already happened.
3. Do not be anxious. Have peace that it will be done.
4. Be thankful.
5. Make your needs and wants known to God.
6. Don't try to figure it out or make sense of how, when, what, or why. Trust God.

What you will do is make a personal prayer list. Not a New Year's resolution or an annual goal list but a personal prayer list.

Become a child—God's little kid, whom he loves so much and wants to make happy. He wants to see you laugh and play. He wants to see you not worried or stressed. Ask your little-kid self what would make you happy. What is it you want? What would give you peace and make you smile? What would get rid of the stress and strife in your life?

Let down your walls that were built by money, people, opportunities, or impossibilities. This is God. You may think you know, but you don't know.

Here is how my personal prayer list usually looks. I break it down into categories.

1. People—those I love and want God to protect, provide for, and connect with; the people I worry about and wish I could follow around and be their guardian angel. But what could I

do? Why not turn that job over to God? So I list whoever I can think of and want to focus on—usually family and friends and then anyone I want to come to know Jesus.

2. Me—I list things about myself, emotional, spiritual, and health. For example, help me fight depression. Help me control my temper. Fill me with joy despite any circumstances. Make me a good wife, mother, and friend. Keep me close to you, God, and connected to you. Give me peace with all people, and keep me smiling and laughing with a positive outlook. Protect me and keep me healthy and strong.

3. Money—I list my financial needs, and I don't hold back. Such as, pay off my car. Pay off my house. Pay off my credit cards. Pay off my student loans. I list the amounts too, exactly what I owe and to whom.

4. Spouse—I list things about my husband. Give him a good job. Help him with his anger and give him patience. Keep him healthy. It helps to turn my spouse's issues over to God, to stop battling him myself, and to realize that God has more power than either of us. He can heal and strengthen any relationship. He can protect it as well.

5. Children—I pray for my son. I want him to be a great man one day. I want to do my part, but I need God's help. This world is horrible. I can't always be there for him. I don't have the control or power needed to protect my innocent little boy. My son is my heart and to put God in charge is very important. Make it known.

6. Personal—here I list things that are just about me. For example, learn to surf. Get better at playing guitar. Start a band. Get my body back in shape. Start sewing. Turn whatever you want over to God. Let him help carve out the time and give you the opportunity. When you look back on your life, these things will not be time wasted. They will make your face light up and, in turn, bring God joy, as you will give him the credit for becoming who you want to be. It's an awesome thing.

7. Outrageous—here is where I list whatever I think is too shocking to even mention, but it might be something such as, I want to tear this house down and build a new one. I want to go to Hawaii for a month's vacation. I want a sailboat. I want a new car. It's usually something I do want, but I'm not sure how or why God would provide it. Or it's something that would be very hard to get on my own. It's just pure joy for my life and probably completely unnecessary, but he's God, and he loves me. He's part of my life (yours too), and this is his show. Let him decide what can and can't be done.

I create a list every year, and I pray over it every day. In the first year, it was September before things on my list started showing up. Then it just went crazy, and God pulled through on almost everything, even some outrageous stuff.

The first thing that got my attention was that I received a commission check that totaled almost exactly the amount of all my financial pay-offs. I knew for a fact that God had just answered my prayer. I had been praying every day for the same thing for nearly nine months, and I didn't doubt that God had come through for me. To say I was shocked, excited, and grateful is an understatement. I paid off *all* of my debt in one fell swoop. What seemed ridiculous and impossible was suddenly finished, just like that. The desire of my heart was delivered. God blessed me. I owe thanks only to him.

If I hadn't made that personal prayer list, prayed every day, and handed all my needs, wants, worries, and so on over to God, I can't imagine what might have transpired. Maybe I would have made money but not spent it wisely. Maybe I wouldn't have made money at all. Either way, I did make money, and I did have the desire of my heart fulfilled right before my eyes.

That's not all. I prayed for a sailboat and got it. I prayed for a surfboard and got it. I prayed for a surfing trip and spent two weeks in Costa Rica. I prayed for my family, and they all had good years. I prayed for my boyfriend (now my husband), and even he was blessed.

I crossed out things on my list, one by one, and watched God do amazing things in my life out of pure love for me. What a great feeling. I look at the things I have, like my Jeep and sailboat, which are things that I own because of God, and I know I owe them to the Lord. I know he gave them to me, and I thank him for that. I don't possess them. They belong to him and his mighty power.

Of course I can't say what will happen for you, but I can testify that year after year, through my personal prayer list, I've seen wonders. I can look back and see what God has done for me—the blessings as well as the hardships for which he has come through for me, year after year.

We often quickly forget and move on. We are quick to get caught up in the next drama or life situation and sometimes forget what God has already done, which makes it hard to keep faith in the moment. But having papers with written proof of God's faithfulness to me and written proof of his love is a huge reminder, particularly in the bad times, that God is here. It makes it easy to believe whatever I need is already handled, so there's no reason to be anxious.

I also believe that by writing a list and keeping that paper with you holds you accountable to communicating with God and giving him your burdens. Trust him to clear your path, to move mountains, to destroy enemies, and to uncover the treasures that are in store for you. It usually takes me twenty to thirty minutes to get through my prayer list. That's time I spend talking to God. Having a list of things helps me from getting distracted, and it keeps me pushing everything his way, which is what he wants. Remember that God doesn't want you to be on your own. He wants to be involved. This is a way to get him involved and to let him do what he wants to do in your life.

Make a list, and give it a try. Make the desires of your heart known to God. Making a prayer list is a point-blank list of things for which you intend to give God credit. Don't tell yourself that you are not good enough for God to answer your prayers. I wasn't living right, and God answered my prayers. God's love for you goes beyond your flaws. Please open your heart to receive the love he has for you. Once you start to get answers to your prayers, you'll praise God and glorify him as never before.

I know God will come through for you because God loves you.

"And this is the confidence that we have in him, that, if we ask any thing according to his will, he heareth us: And if we know that he hear us, whatsoever we ask, we know that we have the petitions that we desired of him" (1 John 5:14–15).

"Wherefore he saith, God resisteth the proud, but giveth grace unto the humble" (James 4:6).

"Therefore I will look unto the LORD; I will wait for the God of my salvation: my God will hear me" (Micah 7:7).

"Cast thy burden upon the LORD, and he shall sustain thee: he shall never suffer the righteous to be moved" (Psalm 55:22).

"Beloved, I wish above all things that thou mayest prosper and be in health, even as thy soul prospereth" (3 John 2).

"'For I know the plans that I have for you,' declares the LORD, 'plans for welfare and not for calamity to give you a future and a hope'" (Jeremiah 29:11).

MY BIG MOUTH 4

There have been so many times in my life when I've thought, *Why can't you just keep your mouth shut? Why did you say that?*

I can tell myself not to say anything, and then *boom*—it just all flows out. Then I feel bad because I couldn't even be true to my own decision to just keep my words to myself. The mouth is a very powerful tool and controls everything.

The following scriptures give a very good description of the power of our tongues and the evil that lies there.

> For in many things we offend all. If any man offend not in word, the same *is* a perfect man, *and* able also to bridle the whole body. Behold, we put bits in the horses' mouths, that they may obey us; and we turn about their whole body. Behold also the ships, which though *they be* so great, and *are* driven of fierce winds, yet are they turned about with a very small helm, whithersoever the governor listeth. Even so the tongue is a little member, and boasteth great things. Behold, how great a matter a little fire kindleth! And the tongue *is* a fire, a world of iniquity: so is the tongue among our members, that it defileth the whole body, and setteth on fire the course of nature; and it is set on fire of hell. For every kind of beasts, and of birds, and of serpents, and of things in the sea, is tamed, and hath been tamed of mankind: But the tongue can no

man tame; *it is* an unruly evil, full of deadly poison. (James 2:2–8)

I love the analogy of our tongues being like the helm of a ship. It's what we use to steer our lives. That is a powerful thing. It's what we use for control. We use our mouths to guide us to the places we want to go. We are the captains of our lives, and our jobs are to control the helms of our ships. But as the verse says, we can tame all the animals and beasts of the world, but no one can tame the tongue. It's an unruly evil, full of deadly poison. A great captain is able to embark on a journey to a specific destination and arrive safely. He plans well in advance and prepares according to the weather, the seas, the crew, and the supplies. He plots and navigates along the way, keeping his crew and himself safe and sound. It takes that same thought, planning, and continuous navigating to keep our lives on course. It takes controlling our tongues.

We all are faced with evil. Evil was released into the world when Adam and Eve ate the forbidden fruit, so we *all* live with it.

"Behold, I was shapen in iniquity; and in sin did my mother conceive me" (Psalm 51:5).

"For [there is] not a just man upon earth, that doeth good, and sinneth not" (Ecclesiastes 7:20).

"For all have sinned, and come short of the glory of God" (Romans 3:23).

"As it is written, There is none righteous, no, not one" (Romans 3:10).

"If we say that we have not sinned, we make him a liar, and his word is not in us" (1 John 1:10).

Don't allow yourself to believe that you are always good because that would be a lie. Therefore, if we all have sinned, then maybe the struggle is not between who is evil and who is good. The struggle is in trying to keep our mouths shut. Personally, my mouth can misrepresent what's in my heart from time to time. Some people, however, have incredible control over their mouths and represent themselves very well.

"Not that which goeth into the mouth defileth a man; but that which cometh out of the mouth, this defileth a man" (Matthew 15:11).

The above verse is super-true for me. My mouth defiles me.

The following verse is the way to correct the problem.

"Let your speech *be* always with grace, seasoned with salt, that ye may know how ye ought to answer every man" (Colossians 4:6).

"Be always with grace"—let's think about this. What would it be like if we were always with grace, if we took our time and stayed true to the decisions we made in advance about what we said. What would it be like if we held our tongues, if we controlled our mouths and only said positive, loving, graceful, wise things? Evil would be severely restricted.

"A good man out of the good treasure of his heart bringeth forth that which is good; and an evil man out of the evil treasure of his heart bringeth forth that which is evil: for of the abundance of the heart his mouth speaketh" (Luke 6:45).

When we say things to others, whether our friends, spouses, children, someone at work or church, or the lady in front of us at the store, we engage in an action/reaction scenario. We have started something that could be good or bad. What we say will determine the reaction from the listener. That reaction might be big or small. The reaction might end right there, or it might carry on. Our mouths have so much more power than we realize. Our level of authority or credibility doesn't matter. Our mouths have enormous power.

For instance, the president of the United States could say to you, "You're a lowlife," and a neighborhood kid could say the same thing, and the sting would be the same. You can shape the outcome of any situation by choosing what comes out of your mouth. As the above verse says, a good man brings good treasure, and an evil man brings out evil treasure. We all battle between good and evil. We all have to check ourselves at times. We do have the ability to choose, and it's important to make good choices. Consider this:

You are at the grocery store and see a young woman with her three small children. Two are in the cart, one is hanging on her, and all three are loud and fussy. She's reading the label on the milk carton as you pass by. You don't know what her day has been like. All you know is that you need some milk, and her kids need a bath. Your eyes are taking it all in as she turns to look at you. The words that come from your mouth will impact the outcome of her day and, more important, her small children's day.

Scenario 1: Your discomfort is clear as you ease slowly toward the milk, saying sternly, "Excuse me." You look over to ensure you make no body contact with the little ones. She waits as you get what you need, and then she moves back to her position to choose the milk best suited for her small children. Meanwhile, she can't help feeling that she and her small children are a nuisance and are disruptive, so she just puts the milk in the cart and moves on down the aisle. In her head is a voice that says her kids are "bad kids" and that people are looking at her like she's a bad mom. Her mood slowly becomes anxious and impatient. Her kids continue to be rowdy as they root through the cart, asking if they can have this or that. Finally, she whispers fiercely that he'd better be quiet, or he'll get a spanking when they get to the car. He cries, which causes the smallest one to cry, so she threatens to put back the candy she had agreed to buy when they were in the first aisle.

You look back at her and her now-crying children and their dismay. She pushes on, putting back the candy and later stuffing her kids into the car, yelling at them on the way home because of this disrupted trip to the grocery store. She feels guilty as they arrive home, with the kids in tears. She sits in the driveway for a few extra minutes. She looks at the faces of her precious babies and takes a deep breath, thinking, *Why did I put the candy back? What went wrong?*

Scenario 2: You look at the young mother, and she catches your smile. You wait as she reads the label on the milk, and you look down at the little boy hanging on her leg. You say, "You must really love your mommy. I bet she's a really good mommy. Are these your brothers?" The little boy smiles and nods his head. You say, "I bet you are a really good big brother, aren't you?" Again, the little boy nods his head and smiles. His mom is smiling too as she watches the interaction between you and her beautiful son. You say to her, "You have beautiful children. You must be the proudest mommy on the planet." She stands up straight with a grin and pulls the little guy hugging her leg closer to her. "I couldn't be any more proud if I tried," she says. "These boys are my whole life." She puts the milk into the cart as she lovingly rubs the shoulders of the oldest child. As you get your milk, you see her kiss the cheek of the middle child, who's smiling, with his candy clenched tightly in his hands. Later on, in the next aisle you hear the crying of the little baby behind you, so you glance back to look. Though the chaos of three small kids carries on, she calmly and happily raises the baby from the cart, kissing his little cheeks. His cries turn into giggles, and your heart warms to see the love between her and her little rascals.

Forest fires can destroy thousands of acres of woods and burn through towns. Just one small match can start such a fire. Think about how small the flame is on a match. Yet it can ignite a fire that spreads until it results in devastating destruction. Don't be that match that goes into the world, looking for stuff to burn down. Instead, be a small puff of air that blows it out or that little drop of water that destroys its ability to do anything.

A seed that grows a massive tree is small. Just a little bitty seed becomes an amazingly beautiful tree. All you have to do is plant it.

Most things—good or bad—start out small. More than likely, they start with small words that may not have much substance at the time. Whether they take root or start a fire, you may never know.

In public, in our homes, or at work, what we send out into the world is either a seed or a match. We are planting seeds that bring good, or we are tossing matches that bring destruction. It all comes from our mouths.

We must mentally, emotionally, and spiritually filter our mouths. We must decide what will and won't be spoken. Then we must stay true to that decision. Our mouths hold too much power for us to not use them with precise and relentless care. We all must learn. I'm still working on that battle between good and evil when it comes to my mouth, but I'm getting better every day.

If we use our mouths as if they are water, we can be more productive. If someone has planted a seed, we should water it and help it to grow. If someone has thrown out a lit match, we should use water to put it out. Use your mouth for God's love. When you don't know what to say, say "God loves you." Those words are like opening a dam. Then say, "And there's nothing anyone can do about it." Most people enjoy that because at some point, someone has made them feel that they aren't good enough to be loved by God.

When you don't know what to say, say, "Jesus loves us, and that's where I find my hope." Say, "You are doing a great job." Say something about love and happiness. Wear a smile on your face. Don't be afraid to tell people that God loves them and that they are doing a great job at life. No one is perfect at it, and we all have times when we are going through some stuff. We just have to be there for one another to help each other focus on the light at the end of the tunnel and to cling to the love God has for us.

We must be prepared to speak good from our hearts because evil is anxiously waiting to come spewing out. When you read the next verse, remember these two words: meekness and fear.

"But sanctify the Lord God in your hearts: and *be* ready always to *give* an answer to every man that asketh you a reason of the hope that is in you with meekness and fear" (Peter 3:15).

It doesn't say "with pride and confidence." There's a reason why God says "with meekness and fear."

JUDGMENT WORDS

5

Have you ever been asked a *destination question*? This is the term I use for a question someone asks, just to strap you in for a ride to the destination he or she has in mind. There may have been a time when your spouse or your parent asked you a question, even though he or she already knew the answer. The person asked the question because he or she wanted to force you into confessing something—something of which the questioner was already well aware. He or she knew the destination (where the conversation was headed) and already had thought out the points he or she wanted to make. People sometimes use destination questions to put people down or to provoke conflict. (I call this speaking evil *gently*.) We need to constantly battle between the good and evil in our hearts. We try to choose good, even though we sometimes don't realize evil is trickling out. Let's look at an example:

Let's say your best friend went out last night, but you didn't—maybe you weren't invited or you already had plans. You saw pictures on social media of all the fun your friend had. You feel left out, especially because you saw another person in the pictures who you don't really like. (Since you weren't there, this person was invited.) You don't say anything to your friend. You don't acknowledge that you saw the pictures. Instead, you ask your friend a destination question: "Who went out with you last night?"

You figure if your friend doesn't feel bad for hanging out with your "frenemy," at least you can get that jab in by making him or her admit to hanging out with that hater. You've used an indirect way to provoke conflict or at least to cause your friend to feel guilty. You haven't yelled or cursed or name-called, but you still have spewed out evil rather than good. You may have been sneaky about it, but it doesn't change the outcome. Good is good. Evil is evil. It doesn't matter how you bring it forth.

Don't use destination questions to try to hide the evil in your heart. It doesn't work. Just because you are soft-spoken and sweet when you speak doesn't mean you are bringing good into the world. It just means you are bringing evil into the world *gently*. This type of passive-aggressive behavior is like pouring salt on a wound. To me, it says, "Oh, you're angry, but you want to provoke me to act out. You want me to look like the bad guy."

It's much more beneficial for both you and your friend to be honest and straightforward. Let your friend know what is going on in your head. It's the only way to deal with a situation. If you manipulate your friend with a destination question, he or she will have to try to figure out the point of the conversation. Your friend may think at first that the two of you are having a nice chat, but it turns out you're prying, provoking, and rerouting the whole talk. You may think you're being clever, but it's evil.

However, you can use destination questions to promote joy and love. Let's say you found out through the grapevine that your friend got a promotion at a work. You are so excited and proud of her. When you see her, you ask, "How's work going?" You know the answer, but you give her the opportunity to share her accomplishment with you. She also will get to see your reaction of joy and love for her in knowing that she is doing well. You get to celebrate with her. Use destination questions for *good*.

Another passive-aggressive type of speech is using what I call *judgment words*. This is when you don't say something obviously insulting, but you do it in a subtle way. However, the person to whom you speak judgment words will understand the link to your judgment, and he or she likely will feel offended and insulted. Regardless of the method you use to insult someone, you are spewing evil from your mouth. And using disclaimers such as "I had no idea," "You took it the wrong way," or "That's not what I meant at all" makes absolutely no difference to the person you've hurt—your judgment was clear.

You can hurt someone without actually saying mean stuff. Let's say you come to see piles of dirty clothes and ask your wife a destination question. "Did you get the laundry done? No? Oh, wow." Here, *wow* is a small judgment word with a big punch to the face. No, you didn't curse, yell, or say anything bad, but the implication is clear. When you follow a destination question with a judgment word, you've given an insult—a recipe for disaster.

Your wife may be about to blow up. She's been chasing three kids all day, paid the bills, vacuumed, and still hasn't finished cleaning the mess from lunch. She didn't make it to the grocery because the baby threw up all over the car. She could not care less about the laundry right now.

What if you didn't use a judgment word but instead said something like, "What can I do to help?" or even "That's okay"? Wouldn't that create a different scenario?

People know when they don't meet your expectations. If you react in a negative or sarcastic way, it's like kicking them when they are down. It's important to be conscious of how you respond and react to an answer. Love is always the right response.

Don't use judgment words to communicate a message that you wouldn't say outright. If you wouldn't say, "Honey, you are not good at being a mom or wife," then don't say it using judgment words.

Apply that to all the relationships and situations you have in your life. When your mouth is moving, one of two things will result: good or evil. Be decisive about which you want to project. There is no reason to hide or try to be gently evil. If you are not encouraging, supporting, loving, and having good purpose in your speech, the consequence will be an evil one. Bad provokes bad. You can't get away with speaking evil. Evil may *sneak* out through judgment words or destination questions, but it's still evil.

As the receiver of a destination question, resist the temptation to fire back.

Though judgment words may seem innocent, using them could be the difference between a good relationship and a not-so-good one. Avoid using the following in judgment: Oh. Huh. Hmmm. Wow. Really? Seriously? Nice. Interesting.

When you ask a destination question, you now drive the conversation. The passenger is the person you are questioning. Be sure that you are driving your passenger carefully and with love.

> Out of the same mouth proceedeth blessing and cursing. My brethren, these things ought not so to be. Doth a fountain send forth at the same place sweet *water* and bitter? Can the fig tree, my brethren, bear olive berries? either a vine, figs? so *can* no fountain both yield salt water and fresh. Who *is* a wise man and endued with knowledge among you? let him shew out of a good conversation his works with meekness of wisdom. But if ye have bitter envying and strife in your hearts, glory not, and lie not against the truth. This wisdom descendeth not from above, but *is* earthly, sensual, devilish. For where envying and strife *is*, there *is* confusion and every evil work. But the wisdom that is from above is first pure, then peaceable, gentle, *and* easy to be intreated, full of mercy and good fruits, without partiality, and without hypocrisy. And the fruit of righteousness is sown in peace of them that make peace. (James 3:10–18)

NO WRONG WAY

6

I've been told to be discerning, realizing that people can be misleading when it comes to what the Bible says. Any time I see something that involves God—a service at a church, a television show, or just a stranger on the street—I start judging. It's like I was appointed by God to determine whether or not the people of the world, who are sacrificing their days and time on earth to work and serve the Lord, are doing it right. It's as if it's up to me to watch them, listen to them, and critique them. I don't do it in a cruel way, but there isn't much good in it.

I won't support lies. I want all religious services backed by scripture. I want truth, as we all do, and I'm responsible for my own salvation. I need to do my due diligence, but I'm talking about my straight-up judgment of other people's work that they do for God. I have been very guilty of it, but recently, I had an epiphany with regard to the Spirit of the Lord, the Holy Ghost, the Holy Spirit.

"And the spirit of the LORD shall rest upon him, the spirit of wisdom and understanding, the spirit of counsel and might, the spirit of knowledge and of the fear of the LORD" (Isaiah 11:2).

"But the Comforter, [which is] the Holy Ghost, whom the Father will send in my name, he shall teach you all things, and bring all things to your remembrance, whatsoever I have said unto you" (John 14:26).

"Likewise the Spirit also helpeth our infirmities: for we know not what we should pray for as we ought: but the Spirit itself maketh intercession for us with groanings which cannot be uttered" (Romans 8:26).

Sometimes this "spirit stuff" can be overwhelming at first. If you are a religious person who talks to your not-so-religious friends about spirits and serpents, they may be ready to run for the hills. It's way too involved for us to ever be able to fathom it while we're in this earthly world. It's a big deal, and I have no clue what's going on beyond this life. I like to think that God has given us a glimpse, but it's barely visible. I have read about the Holy Ghost (or Holy Spirit) enough to know that it exists. I have had my own thoughts and ideas, later confirmed by scripture. I have learned that these thoughts were actually the Spirit of the Lord giving me wisdom—wisdom that I was not taught in a class or that I read about on my own.

As the above verses describe, the Holy Ghost (Holy Spirit) is a good thing. This is the guy who will keep you out of trouble. He will be your wisdom, understanding, counsel, might, knowledge, fear of God, comforter, teacher, rememberer, helper, and communicator,

Yes, I'll take one, please. I could certainly wise up a little. I can definitely use some help, and he will help me remember things. I definitely need that. And he will do all the communicating for me. That's awesome.

I wish I could see my Holy Spirit. I wish we could grab coffee each morning and discuss the day. He would be my life coach, and I would be his good student. Unfortunately, that's not how it works, but it isn't too far off.

"In whom ye also [trusted], after that ye heard the word of truth, the gospel of your salvation: in whom also after that ye believed, ye were sealed with that Holy Spirit of promise" (Ephesians 1:13).

Have you realized that Jesus actually existed? He was a man on earth. He was God's son. Yes, he died, and you are now forgiven for all of your sins forever. Because of that, you are going to heaven. Once you accept this, God looks at you with a happy heart and tells one of his mighty and trusted *holy spirits* to take care of you.

All of a sudden, without even knowing it or making any requests, you have a life coach. You have someone who will speak to you when you are not sure about things. When you are exposed to something that isn't in line with what God had in mind, your coach will make the correction in your mind without your knowing. When you pray to God but aren't making any sense, your coach will step in and talk to God on your behalf. Your coach will be your filter for all things that come in and go out of your mind and heart. It's great.

There have been times when I have "known" things, even though I wasn't sure why I knew them or understood how it works when it comes to God and this whole forgiveness bit. I just thought I was smart and maybe had a gift of intuition. I have thought certain things and then later had them confirmed by scripture, and I've told myself I was smart. But it wasn't me at all. It was the guy in my ear, telling me what's up.

I think about the unfortunate people around the globe who don't have the opportunity to go to a church service, read a book, or meet with a teacher to learn about God and Jesus. I believe they only need to be introduced to and then believe in Jesus Christ as their Savior. The Holy Spirit will come to them and teach them everything they need to know. Reading the Bible isn't necessary for salvation, but reading the Bible will support what the Holy Spirit, God, and Jesus are trying to accomplish in your life, so don't deprive yourself of that. It's important.

It's in knowing that the Holy Spirit will discern and judge, on my behalf, all information taken into my mind and heart that I can have peace when I go to a worship service or listen to a pastor. I can enjoy the love of God displayed by others. I can praise God freely and encourage others to continue their efforts to praise God freely.

"The Lord will perfect that which concerneth me: thy mercy, O Lord, endureth forever: forsake not the works of thine own hands" (Psalm 138:8).

Can God make it any clearer? He will perfect that which concerns me.

I have realized that I am not appointed to judge other people who try to glorify God with their service, whatever it may be. If people want to ride naked on a broom with "Jesus Loves Me" tattooed on their backs for the glory of God, I won't judge them. I'll say "Praise the Lord! There's somebody who's crazy about God!" I may never join in, but I won't judge because I know God will perfect that which concerns me and those people as well.

My husband and I have been searching for a church in our town. He wants to hear a deep biblical study-type sermon that feeds believers and develops them as Christians. I like singing and praising God and lots of action. I like to see a church that's working hard for God in the community and that's chasing after unbelievers. So we started bouncing around town, looking for the right fit. One church had a good message every day, good music, and always wrapped things up with the good news of Jesus Christ. My husband, however, still was not getting the depth he wanted.

We visited another church with the in-depth study that my husband wanted. They went through the entire Bible in a year. He was ecstatic. As we continued to attend this church, however, we started to see the internal drama. The last service we attended was like a board meeting with rules on being late and how to dress. *No, thank you*, I thought. Besides, the music was boring.

My friend invited me to a church that fit all the needs I had—music, community, action, opportunities to serve the Lord. I was so excited. But when my husband attended, he was not impressed. I worried that we never would find the right church.

Throughout this process of searching, though, I realized something. There was never one moment where I stopped to appreciate the works of the people running the churches. We'd go to the service and then just bash them on the car ride home. I immediately identified what they were doing wrong. Every preacher was messing up. Every band needed to switch it up. Every congregation was weak. Even the parking lots were wrong. It was like no one could get it right.

The devil had corrupted my mind so much that I couldn't even acknowledge or appreciate—let alone glorify—God in the moments he deserved it.

Then I witnessed it again. I took some friends to church; they had never been to a large church, and it was a total culture shock for them. Everything was different, and later the comments flowed out of them. The church wasn't doing this or that. "They didn't quote the verse accurately. That's not right." I got it. There is a correct way, a way that is not affected by sin. It, however, does not exist on this earth. We have to trust God. We have stop overanalyzing and start worshiping. As Christians, we are so busy criticizing and critiquing the acts of other Christians that we don't give any glory to God.

Rather than be critical of the service, why not rejoice in the number of people who showed up to worship God? Praise God for loving you and accepting you. Trust the Holy Spirit, and know that God loves you, Jesus saved you, the Holy Spirit is guiding you, and there is nothing anyone can do to change that.

We have to keep clinging to this verse: "The Lord will perfect that which concerneth me: thy mercy, O Lord, endureth forever: forsake not the works of thine own hands" (Psalm 138:8).

I have a hard time believing that all the people in the church or all the preachers or those who started a church are in it for the money. *Greed—they just want your money. They are desecrating the Word of God and everything Jesus stands for. Avoid the churches! They are all evil.*

Even though there have been times in life when I did believe this, I now realize that is what the devil wants me to believe. It's what he wants *all* of us to believe, even those who love God and believe Jesus died for them. He wants to separate the church from the world— push it out and make people perceive them as bad.

My dad sang at church and played guitar. Meanwhile, I wanted to be a country music singing superstar, and that was a lot of pressure for my dad. My dad tried hard to support me, help me, and be there for me.

Unfortunately, the church did not. I had landed a gig at the casino, which was probably my biggest gig ever. The church said my dad couldn't play at the casino on Saturday and at church on Sunday. It just didn't "look good."

That didn't go over well with me. I knew what we were doing wasn't bad. I thought that every time we took the stage as a family (my uncle played bass), God tuned in for the show. He loved us. He still does. The church, however, tried to dictate what was *good* and *not good*.

This made me sad. God finally had my dad—his wonderful, gifted child—standing at the altar, worshiping with his blessed voice and talented music, but this church said, "You have to quit." I'm sure God was not pleased to see my dad pack up his guitar and stop playing music in the church.

Can you imagine a church that turns away people who aren't living the way the church thinks they should live? Is the church only for people who only live a certain lifestyle? It just doesn't make sense to me. We know that there is not one person who can rise above the sins of this world, so who exactly are we trying to have attend our church? *No one?*

It's like when people say, "Repent! Turn from your sinful ways and come to God!" That is *not*, however, how it works. If you are battling a sin, then you won't defeat that sin without God. How are you supposed to "turn from your sinful ways" and *then* "come to God"? That's backwards. What people should be saying is, "Turn to God. He loves you! He will help you defeat the sins that control you."

I think the church was okay in saying they needed to get my dad out of the casino. Where they went wrong was in turning my dad away from what might have been God's plan for him—and who knows? Maybe even me. They should have given it over to God. Once they identified the issue of playing music at the casino, they should have turned to God with prayer, saying, for example, "Wouldn't it be great if his family band sang songs for the glory of God? Wouldn't it be great if the daughter wanted to be a gospel singer? Let's start praying for God to do his will in their lives. We know he loves them and has blessed them with this wonderful gift and passion for music. Let's pray that God will work in their lives to do what he has planned for them."

They should have followed through with those prayers and could have openly talked about that with my dad, with enthusiasm and acceptance and love. He would have been happy to know that he and his family were being prayed for. And probably he would have praised and worshipped in song on Sunday with more glory to God than ever before.

Of course, that's not what happened. My dad still has not attended a church regularly, nor has he participated in any musical praise at a church. That's sad. It was the church's judgment and decision that turned him away. I'm guilty too, though. We all are at some point. We have to pull it together and stop trying to be so controlling and dictating what is right or wrong, offering our "invaluable" advice to others. Instead, we have to give it to God. We have to pray. We have to respect the power of prayer. The greatest action we can take in others' lives is *praying* for them.

"Confess [your] faults one to another, and pray one for another, that ye may be healed. The effectual fervent prayer of a righteous man availeth much" (James 5:16).

"Be careful for nothing; but in every thing by prayer and supplication with thanksgiving let your requests be made known unto God" (Philippians 4:6).

"For this cause we also, since the day we heard [it], do not cease to pray for you, and to desire that ye might be filled with the knowledge of his will in all wisdom and spiritual understanding" (Colossians 1:9).

"But I say unto you, Love your enemies, bless them that curse you, do good to them that hate you, and pray for them which despitefully use you, and persecute you" (Matthew 5:44).

"Again I say unto you, That if two of you shall agree on earth as touching any thing that they shall ask, it shall be done for them of my Father which is in heaven" (Matthew 18:19)

"Now I beseech you, brethren, for the Lord Jesus Christ's sake, and for the love of the Spirit, that ye strive together with me in [your] prayers to God for me" (Romans 15:30).

"Brethren, pray for us" (1 Thessalonians 5:25).

"And this I pray, that your love may abound yet more and more in knowledge and [in] all judgment" (Philippians 1:9–11).

"Finally, brethren, pray for us, that the word of the Lord may have [free] course, and be glorified, even as [it is] with you" (2 Thessalonians 3:1).

If people are in the world doing things because they love God, they are not doing it the wrong way. If you feel someone is being distracted or confused by Satan, take action by *praying* for him or her. Remember that God will perfect that which concerns you and me and everyone else. Satan is successful at creating a wall between the church and the world. That wall is what keeps people from turning to God. It keeps people from ever being rescued from the doubt and belief that God doesn't love them.

The media is so good at building walls between the religious and the rest of the world. Stop going along with it. Who are you to say who is and isn't loved by God? Who are you to say what does and doesn't glorify God? I think God was glorified when my dad played those old gospel tunes for him at church on Sundays. I don't think he was glorified when my dad was asked to stop.

My dad likely will never play in a church again, unless there's some miracle. The cold, hard truth is that evil exists everywhere. It is up to us to let *God* deal with it. And this statement is highly directed to members of the church: *let God deal with it. Pray. Don't push people away. Pray. Pray. Pray.*

"The Lord will perfect that which concerneth me: thy mercy, O Lord, endureth forever: forsake not the works of thine own hands" (Psalm 138:8).

Note: As I was writing this chapter, my dad told me that he was invited by a friend to sing at his church. Coincidence? I think not. My dad went, and he did stand at the altar and sing praises to God—that miracle took place. After nearly twenty years, God perfected that which concerneth him. It makes me laugh because my dad had no idea that I used his story as an example in my book. Yet God presented that opportunity to him precisely at the time I was writing it. I believe it was just to reconfirm to me that God perfects all things. He has *all* power and control. I think God also is telling me to let it go. What I think is a big deal is not a big deal to God. If it were, my dad would be at the altar singing every Sunday because God clearly can make anything happen that he sees fit.

Just as I am guilty of judging other believers, I know that someone right now is judging me and has been judging me from the very beginning. All I know, however, is that I love God, and he loves me. Guess what? He loves you. I'm not perfect and don't want to pretend that I am. I'm a real person with real problems, and I make real mistakes. For whatever reason, God has put it on my heart to write this book, and he laid it on me thick. If you have an issue with that, take it up with God, but know that this book was written for the glory of God. I love God. Everything I do is the *wrong way*, and I do it *all* wrong for the glory of God, knowing that he will perfect that which concerns me.

I know if I give him the honor and glory of the things I do, he will perfect it. I know he is perfecting the works of others who love and honor him. I know they are going to do it the wrong way too. And I know I'm going to love them, support them, and praise and love God right along with them, no matter how they go about it.

"For all have sinned, and come short of the glory of God" (Romans 3:23).

We will never do justice to the Lord Almighty. Even if you started a church, led a worship, sang every Sunday, and wrote the message, you would do it the wrong way too. We all fall short. So if that's the case, we have to stop judging other believers. I know that in writing this book, I will be judged, mostly by other believers. In that judgment and critiquing, I ask that you will pray for me and this book.

Let's start glorifying God in all the things we do and in all the things others do. We all fall short of the glory of God, and only God can perfect that which concerns God. No one will ever serve, worship, teach, or lead people to God the *right* way, simply because we are all tarnished by sin in everything we do. The only thing we can do for one another that is right is to pray.

THE RICH

7

"For the love of money is the root of all evil" (1 Timothy 6) —the *love* of money. Segregate that in your mind from money itself. *Loving* money is evil. Money is just money.

"For it is easier for a camel to go through a needle's eye, than for a rich man to enter into the kingdom of God" (Luke 18:25).

I remember my preacher preaching on this verse many years ago. As a child, I was very confused—I knew a camel would never fit through the eye of a needle. So what I heard is that a rich man will not ever enter the kingdom of God (heaven). On that day at church, I was heartbroken. I wanted to be a country music star, entertainer of the year, and get a trophy. I wanted to have my name in lights and be ... well, rich. But I'd just learned that if that happened, I couldn't go to Heaven. I was really conflicted and sad—and confused. Why would God let me want to be a singer if that meant I would be rich, and that meant I wouldn't go to heaven? This was too much for that time in my life, but I never forgot it.

Later, in a Bible study, I asked about this verse. I then learned that in biblical times the people referred to the side gate of the city—which was small and harder to pass through—as the "eye of the needle." Camels would have to kneel down and crawl through the gate.

The following is information I found online:

> Used only in the proverb, "to pass through a needle's eye" (Matthew 19:24; Mark 10:25; Luke 18:25).

Some interpret the "expression as referring to the side gate, close to the principal" "gate, usually called the "eye of a needle" in the East; but it" is rather to be taken literally.

I am unaware of any scripture in the Bible that clarifies this verse and the idea of the side gate. It's up to you to decide. I believe that the next few verses would be unnecessary if it were not true. If Jesus was referring to the eye of a sewing needle, there is no hope for the camel or the rich man. If that were the case, why would he teach how a rich man should be?

The camel has to kneel down and crawl through the gate, which is not easy for a tall, large animal like a camel. I can imagine it would take a lot of effort and would be uncomfortable. Still, on the other side of the gate, the camel would receive food and water and be able to rest, so the camel would drop to its knees and crawl through. This is a great analogy for rich people who easily rely on themselves for their needs, people who perhaps are very proud and have a sense of power here on earth. In order for them to focus on what God has to offer and the end game (death), they will have to take their eyes off of their belongings, or step out of their powerful positions and humble themselves as sinners who need the forgiveness Jesus has to offer—just like the camel kneeling to crawl through the gate.

"But they that will be rich fall into temptation and a snare, and [into] many foolish and hurtful lusts, which drown men in destruction and perdition" (1 Timothy 6:9).

They that be rich fall into temptation. They fall into a snare. They fall into many foolish and hurtful lusts. They drown in destruction and perdition. Why? Because they can afford to do so. Imagine if you had the money to go out every time you wanted. You could go on any vacation or buy all the food and drinks you wanted. I bet things could get out of hand from time to time. Being poor makes being "good" a lot easier. No matter what your flesh (mind and body) wants to do; your wallet often says no.

For a rich person, the wallet is not a dictator for the flesh. The reality is all individuals are subject to the sinful nature and desires of the flesh. Someone who has the money to afford those desires faces another layer of self-control. Relying on ourselves can be a losing battle. As the verse says, "they that will be rich fall into temptation and a snare, and [into] many foolish and hurtful lusts, which drown men in destruction and perdition."

Just because it talks about the rich, however, doesn't mean it excludes the poor. A poor man can fall into the same temptations, if given the opportunity. The verse is just letting a rich man know he needs to be aware, because having the money means having to rely on yourself more to stay out of trouble.

Does it mean that to be rich is bad and to be poor is good? No. It just means being a rich man comes with more opportunities to fall into the temptations, snares, and foolish and hurtful lusts.

"For the love of money is the root of all evil: which while some coveted after, they have erred from the faith, and pierced themselves through with many sorrows" (1 Timothy 6:10).

The following passage is Jesus offering his love to those who have struggled with being rich.

> Because thou sayest, I am rich, and increased with goods, and have need of nothing; and knowest not that thou art wretched, and miserable, and poor, and blind, and naked: I counsel thee to buy of me gold tried in the fire, that thou mayest be rich; and white raiment, that thou mayest be clothed, and *that* the shame of thy nakedness do not appear; and anoint thine eyes with eyesalve, that thou mayest see. As many as I love, I rebuke and chasten: be zealous therefore, and repent. Behold, I stand at the door, and knock: if any man hear my voice, and open the door, I will come in to him, and will sup with him, and he with me. To him that overcometh will I grant to sit with me in my throne, even as I also overcame,

and am set down with my Father in his throne. (Revelation 3:17–21)

Jesus is calling out those who are rich and do not know how wretched, poor, miserable, blind, and naked they are. He's telling them to counsel (talk to him) and take his gold that is "tried by fire." This means he went to hell; he's been through the worst experience imaginable and has never lost value. He is saying he will clothe you in the finest garment of white, and anoint your eyes to see. He is knocking. He wants you to let him in and for you to be with him in heaven because … he loves you.

These are awesome words, especially knowing that even the wealthiest of people have need of Jesus and that *he has need of them*. People who can buy and build whatever they want; those who have need for nothing have need of him.

I love this next passage, and it makes me laugh because it is so true of us humans. We are always trying to make a dollar and planning for the future. We are brought up this way. We go to school, then to college, get a great job, save for retirement, buy investments to make more money for the future, and then die and leave the money to our families.

We do have to plan and be wise—trust me; as I've mentioned, I'm in the financial industry. I see that it makes a difference in your financial future if you do live into old age; you will need money. Just remember that we do not know what tomorrow holds. The future is all whatever God allows it to be.

"Go to now, ye that say, Today or tomorrow we will go into such a city, and continue there a year, and buy and sell, and get gain: Whereas ye know not what *shall be* on the morrow. For what *is* your life? It is even a vapour, that appeareth for a little time, and then vanisheth away. For that ye *ought* to say, If the Lord will, we shall live, and do this, or that" (James 4:13–15).

You may plan your next business move and let that be your life's focus, but your life is but a vapor—here one day and gone the next. Put thought into the fact that this is not going to last forever. Your success, your business, your life—it will end ... and then what? What value are your assets and your accomplishments when you are dead?

"Go to now, *ye* rich men, weep and howl for your miseries that shall come upon *you*. Your riches are corrupted, and your garments are moth eaten. Your gold and silver is cankered; and the rust of them shall be a witness against you, and shall eat your flesh as it were fire. Ye have heaped treasure together for the last days" (James 5:1–3).

Wealth, material things, big houses, cool cars, vacations—they all are great for a short time but then suddenly they lose their appeal. Jesus is saying to you to overcome this love of money and material things and love him instead. He wants you to sit with him at his throne.

"Behold, the hire of the labourers who have reaped down your fields, which is of you kept back by fraud, crieth: and the cries of them which have reaped are entered into the ears of the Lord of sabaoth. Ye have lived in pleasure on the earth, and been wanton; ye have nourished your hearts, as in a day of slaughter. Ye have condemned *and* killed the just; *and* he doth not resist you" (James 5:4–6).

Be sure to take good care of your people because while you sit in your fancy house, eating your fancy food; you don't want them to be begging God to help them buy food for their families. God is taking record of it and you never want to be on the opposing side of God.

"But now ye rejoice in your boastings: all such rejoicing is evil. Therefore to him that knoweth to do good, and doeth *it* not, to him it is sin" (James 4:16–17).

I like this verse about sin. If you know in your heart what the "good thing" to do is, but you don't do it, then you are sinning. Think about it. In some instances a choice may be a sin, and in some cases it might not be. It's all about what is in your heart and the choice you make at the time. Sin is a personal thing. It's not a list of dos and don'ts. It's what God has put in your heart at the time and the decision you make.

If you know that people in your company need more money to survive, yet you refuse to give them raises or pay them fair wages, while you live lavishly and gain more and more, odds are you know in your heart it's wrong. If you continue to choose this way, however, God won't be happy with you. But you know that.

You also should know that there is forgiveness in Jesus Christ. Your sins are no different from any other sin. They are forgivable. Believe in Jesus Christ as the Son of God and that he died on the cross for you too. When you hear God knocking on the door of your heart, let him in. Better yet, call him up, and invite him over. After all, God loves rich people too.

In this next passage, Jesus points out that a poor widow gave all of her money, and the disciples gave and the rich gave. The rich gave a lot, but Jesus lets them know that it isn't necessarily the dollar amount that you give that matters. This lady gave *everything* she had. Even though the dollar amount was small, it was *not* small to her. The rich gave large amounts, but it was minor compared to the poor widow. What is a large sum of money to one person is very little to another. God ultimately knows what's in our hearts. He knows how much we are trying to make a difference. He knows whether it is a lot or not. It depends on us, our situations, and—most important—what's in our hearts.

> And Jesus sat over against the treasury, and beheld how the people cast money into the treasury: and many that were rich cast in much. And there came a certain poor widow, and she threw in two mites, which make a farthing. And he called *unto him* his disciples, and saith unto them, Verily I say unto you, That this poor widow hath cast more in, than all they which have cast into the treasury: For all *they* did cast in of their abundance; but she of her want did cast in all that she had, *even* all her living. (Mark 12:41–44)

God doesn't judge a man based on his net worth, whether good or bad. He doesn't say that because a man has more than five million dollars, he is rich. He doesn't say that because a man earns less than minimum wage, he is poor. What's in your bank account is not going to determine if you are good or evil. It's what's in your heart.

Some people are just arrogant and boastful. They equate their net worth to their worth as a person, and it's how they measure others as well. I have met a lot of people in my life; some were wealthier than others. I grew up on a farm in a very rural area, and my perception of rich back then was very different from today. Living in South Florida near some the wealthiest people in the world, my perception of rich has become a little more developed. The thing that hasn't changed, however, is the knowledge that there is always someone who has more than you. You see people with a certain level of wealth, and you want to get there. Once you do, you see others who have more than you, so you want to get to *that* level. Once you get there, there are still others who you are wealthier, so you want to get to their level. It never ends. Rarely do we just say to ourselves, "We made it," and then let it go.

"But woe unto you that are rich! for ye have received your consolation" (Luke 6:24).

"And he lifted up his eyes on his disciples, and said, Blessed [be ye] poor: for yours is the kingdom of God" (Luke 6:20).

Why does he say the poor are blessed and will inherit the kingdom of God? Because they rely on God for everything—they have to. So they are *blessed* simply because they have one less hurdle to get through in order to have a relationship with God. They don't have to kneel down to crawl through the eye of the needle; they can just walk through the main gate. When a man is rich, he is burdened with a busy lifestyle that's plagued with plans, plans, and more plans. It can be a terrible distraction from God and from the end game (death and heaven). That's why it says, "Woe unto them that are rich."

"No man can serve two masters: for either he will hate the one, and love the other; or else he will hold to the one, and despise the other. Ye cannot serve God and mammon" (Matthew 6:24).

If money is your master, then how can God be your master? Serve God, not the dollar or anything it can buy you. Money cannot buy eternity, eternal peace, lifelong happiness, or freedom from guilt and shame.

"Charge them that are rich in this world, that they be not high-minded, nor trust in uncertain riches, but in the living God, who giveth us richly all things to enjoy" (1 Timothy 6:17).

Think about the above verse deeply. Read it carefully and take it in. To be rich is not to be evil. It does not mean you are not Christlike. Don't be high-minded (arrogant and proud). Don't put your trust in yourself, your accomplishments, or your abilities, and especially not in your money or belongings. For they can all be gone tomorrow. Worse yet, you can be gone tomorrow. Put your trust in God and in Jesus Christ, who loves you. Be proud of the work Jesus did on the cross.

"[Let your] conversation [be] without covetousness; [and be] content with such things as ye have: for he hath said, I will never leave thee, nor forsake thee" (Hebrews 13:5).

This is where faith comes in. The love of money can lead us away from faith in Christ. We need faith. We need to relax and know that God will never leave us high and dry. He won't forsake us, no matter how much or how little we have.

"For the sun is no sooner risen with a burning heat, but it withereth the grass, and the flower thereof falleth, and the grace of the fashion of it perisheth: so also shall the rich man fade away in his ways" (James 1:11).

The material things come and go. I couldn't fit all the clothes and shoes I've bought over the years in my closet right now. I couldn't fit all the cars I've owned over my lifetime in my driveway right now. It comes and goes. I can't even remember half the stuff I've owned in my life. It seems valuable when it's in the moment, but then it fades away. I see myself wearing a certain outfit in old photographs and think, *Whatever happened to that shirt?* I have no clue, even though at one time, it was my favorite shirt. God's love never fades away like that. He doesn't go out of style or diminish over time.

"Lay not up for yourselves treasures upon earth, where moth and rust doth corrupt, and where thieves break through and steal: ...

For where your treasure is, there will your heart be also" (Matthew 6:19, 21).

This life is so miniscule. What are you going to hoard that will make a difference? Be wise. Think about tomorrow, but don't think you are going to accomplish anything by storing treasures on earth. When you die, it will go to someone else.

The next passage is lengthy but worth reading. It shows how much God loves the rich and wants them to come to him. He wants to give them the same wonderful freedom and peace that he has offered to the poor. Christians isolate rich people for the same reason they isolate scriptures—they don't focus on the whole passage. Take time to read this passage and remember that Jesus Christ died for our sins so that we *all* have eternal life, so that we *all* can enter the kingdom of God. Side gate or not, we are getting in there.

> Perverse disputings of men of corrupt minds, and destitute of the truth, supposing that gain is godliness: from such withdraw thyself. But godliness with contentment is great gain. For we brought nothing into *this* world, *and it is* certain we can carry nothing out. And having food and raiment let us be therewith content. But they that will be rich fall into temptation and a snare, and *into* many foolish and hurtful lusts, which drown men in destruction and perdition.
>
> For the love of money is the root of all evil: which while some coveted after, they have erred from the faith, and pierced themselves through with many sorrows. But thou, O man of God, flee these things; and follow after righteousness, godliness, faith, love, patience, meekness. Fight the good fight of faith, lay hold on eternal life, whereunto thou art also called, and hast professed a good profession before many witnesses. I give thee charge in the sight of God, who quickeneth all things, and *before* Christ Jesus, who before Pontius Pilate witnessed a good confession;

That thou keep *this* commandment without spot, unrebukeable, until the appearing of our Lord Jesus Christ: Which in his times he shall shew, *who is* the blessed and only Potentate, the King of kings, and Lord of lords; Who only hath immortality, dwelling in the light which no man can approach unto; whom no man hath seen, nor can see: to whom *be* honor and power everlasting. Amen.

Charge them that are rich in this world, that they be not highminded, nor trust in uncertain riches, but in the living God, who giveth us richly all things to enjoy; That they do good, that they be rich in good works, ready to distribute, willing to communicate; Laying up in store for themselves a good foundation against the time to come, that they may lay hold on eternal life. O Timothy, keep that which is committed to thy trust, avoiding profane *and* vain babblings, and oppositions of science falsely so called: Which some professing have erred concerning the faith. Grace *be* with thee. Amen. (1 Timothy 6:5–21)

A Christian stereotype is to be poor and unsuccessful and not do anything about it. God will provide – and he does. But Satan has used that against us. He has tricked us into accepting laziness.

God brought me into this world with capable hands, feet, a back, and a brain. I can learn, and I can work. I'm not going to sit around and wonder. I'm going to do. I'm going to do what it takes to make the difference. God gave me the tools to do it.

The one thing I won't do is assist in Satan's plan to isolate and manipulate a rich person into believing God and Christians do not love him or her. I will not allow Satan to convince a hard-working, successful, intelligent, driven family to believe that by accepting Jesus Christ as their Lord and Savior means giving up the life they have built for themselves.

If you consider yourself a rich or wealthy individual, this is from

Timothy 6:11–12. God is talking to you when he says, "But thou, O man of God, flee these things; and follow after righteousness, godliness, faith, love, patience, meekness. Fight the good fight of faith, lay hold on eternal life, whereunto thou art also called, and hast professed a good profession before many witnesses."

Fight the good fight of faith and have no shame in your good profession. For God has no shame for you. With you, he is pleased, and he loves you.

"Every man according as he purposeth in his heart, [so let him give]; not grudgingly, or of necessity: for God loveth a cheerful giver" (2 Corinthians 9:7).

"That they do good, that they be rich in good works, ready to distribute, willing to communicate" (1 Timothy 6:18).

AND FAMOUS

8

If you watch the news and shows on TV, they don't seem to be Christian-based. Meanwhile, I shake my head at some of the stuff I see on social media—Christians shaming and pointing the finger at celebrities, shouting out against the acts of others, or condemning everyone they can. Jesus didn't come to condemn the world. He came to save it. Is that really the message we portray and send into the world? Not always, and from my perspective, it's rarely.

I see the shift of the outside world, looking down on Christian behaviors, and it breaks my heart. I can't help but say, "We are doing it to ourselves." We have people out there misrepresenting the love of God, the grace of God, and the sacrifice of Jesus Christ. If we truly stood for the love and forgiveness of everyone in the world, as Jesus did, then how could we be frowned upon? How could we be pushed off the air, show by show? The love, acceptance, and forgiveness that people seek lies with *nonbelievers*. They have more compassion and empathy for people struggling than some Christians. This breaks my heart. It has to change.

I feel like we are so off course as Christians and in the message we send out to the world that I need to go through every possible scenario that might be questionable. Again, let me sum it up for you.

God loves everyone, and there is *nothing* anyone can do about it.

We have to love each other, and God wants everyone to trust in him. God wants everyone to know that he loves everyone. Don't be the voice that keeps someone from trusting God. Don't be the person who keeps others from believing that God loves them.

I've mentioned previously that I wanted to be a country music star for my entire life. It's human nature to have heroes, to be a fan, and to enjoy being entertained by someone in sports, music, acting, or comedy. God created us in his likeness. I believe God enjoys entertainment as much as we do. So why, then, are celebrities swept in to this pool of evil, ungodly folk?

Do you really have to sell your soul to the devil to become famous? Is there a sign-up sheet, and people sign the dotted line? I honestly don't know, but I do know this: Jesus Christ died for everyone, including girls and boys who would do anything to see their dreams come true, people who chased a dream and open up the wrong door and skip down the wrong path or shake the wrong hand. There are no *deals* too big, too deep, too dark, or too outrageous for God. Satan can try to buy whatever he wants, but Jesus has already paid for you. You belong to him.

People talk about a certain celebrity they've seen on TV as if they know this person's whole life story and, more importantly, as if they know what's in the person's heart and what the person's relationship with God looks like.

Just because you can recognize someone's face and have seen that person on television doesn't mean you are tuned in to his or her relationship with God. You have no idea how God is working in his or her life. You have no idea how God is using that person to his good. You have no idea what that person is struggling with. Most importantly, you have no right to judge those people. You do not know them. Even if you were their best friend, you still don't know. Everyone's relationship with God is his or her own.

The more that people slam and judge celebrities in the name of God, the further Christianity will be pushed out of the media and, worse yet, the more nonbelievers will be disgusted by our faith. Besides, that behavior does not represent Jesus Christ or the Bible at all.

That said, I want to highlight a couple of things.

Satan wants to portray Christians as judgmental bullies who dictate what is acceptable and what's not. Don't let him use the media to provoke you, make you lash out in anger, and misrepresent what Jesus came to the world to accomplish. Forgiveness applies to *all*. Be calm and loving to all.

If someone is making choices that are not in line with what you believe are acceptable behaviors, if someone is living a life that is offensive or disgusting to you, pray for that person.

"Let us not therefore judge one another any more: but judge this rather, that no man put a stumbling block or an occasion to fall in his brother's way" (Romans 14:13).

Stop judging one another. Stop dictating what is right or wrong. Pray for one another, for God is mighty to save.

"For God sent not his Son into the world to condemn the world; but that the world through him might be saved" (John 3:17). Jesus doesn't condemn, so why would you? God doesn't want condemnation, so why do you?

"Therefore to him that knoweth to do good, and doeth *it* not, to him it is sin" (James 4:17). What applies to you may not apply to someone else. If you did these things, you would be sinning because you find it bad, but that's you. You don't know this other person's deal with God, what the person knows or doesn't know, or what God has put in his or her heart. It's also not your concern. It's God's, and he will perfect what concerneth you and *him or her*.

God loves everyone. God forgives all things. God never gives up on anyone. We do not get to decide who's in and who's out with God. Represent the love and forgiveness that Jesus gave the world so that all can be saved and all can inherit the kingdom of God.

God loves everyone, and there's nothing anyone can do about it.

ADDICTS

> Judge not, that ye be not judged. For with what
> judgment ye judge, ye shall be judged: and with what
> measure ye mete, it shall be measured to you again.
> And why beholdest thou the mote(spec of saw dust)
> that is in thy brother's eye, but considerest not the
> beam that is in thine own eye? Or how wilt thou say
> to thy brother, Let me pull out the mote out of thine
> eye; and, behold, a beam is in thine own eye? Thou
> hypocrite, first cast out the beam out of thine own
> eye; and then shalt thou see clearly to cast out the
> mote out of thy brother's eye. (Matthew 7:1–5)

Hypocrisy is a huge issue for me and for many people with regard to Christians and the church. The stereotype for a Christian is someone who is a hypocrite and is judgmental. How did this stereotype come to be?

Hypocrisy within the church and among Christians has become a massive divider between believers and nonbelievers. Who would ever want to be labeled as a hypocrite? This image of the stereotypical Christian keeps those seeking hope and refuge from ever exploring the teachings of Jesus Christ. It has also kept those who are capable and willing to serve God from ever doing so; they don't want to subject themselves to these stereotypes.

I believe the issue lies in the social boundaries we have created. As a Christian society, we have decided what behaviors are acceptable and unacceptable. From a biblical standpoint, *all* lines lead to unacceptable. *All fall short of the glory of God.* We are born into sin. The Bible paints a picture of a level playing field when it comes to our sinful natures, yet we continue to divide and decide.

Until we as Christians start responding to all walks of life with God's love, acceptance, and forgiveness, we will continue to battle these stereotypes.

> Beloved, let us love one another: for love is of God; and every one that loveth is born of God, and knoweth God. He that loveth not knoweth not God; for God is love. In this was manifested the love of God toward us, because that God sent his only begotten Son into the world, that we might live through him. Herein is love, not that we loved God, but that he loved us, and sent his Son [to be] the propitiation for our sins. Beloved, if God so loved us, we ought also to love one another.
> (1 John 4:7–11)

To make my point, I want to talk about addictions. The word *addiction* is generally used in a very negative context. No one wants to have an addiction or be an addict. That is a socially unacceptable behavior and usually assumes an addiction to drugs. But what if you are addicted to food? Shopping? Playing video games? Social media? Exercise? Having these "addictions" are easily justified and excused; in fact, they are rarely labeled with the word addiction in the first place. I believe, however, that God sees all things of this world as addictive.

"For all that [is] in the world, the lust of the flesh, and the lust of the eyes, and the pride of life, is not of the Father, but is of the world" (1 John 2:16).

God has come to bring us life abundantly, to give us all good things that are of him. The things of this world rob us of the abundant life God is offering. We are distracted, lured, and addicted to things of this world. What is robbing you of your abundant life?

"The thief cometh not, but for to steal, and to kill, and to destroy: I am come that they might have life, and that they might have [it] more abundantly" (John 10:10).

"For I know the thoughts that I think toward you, saith the LORD, thoughts of peace, and not of evil, to give you an expected end" (Jeremiah 29:11).

"And be not conformed to this world: but be ye transformed by the renewing of your mind, that ye may prove what [is] that good, and acceptable, and perfect, will of God" (Romans 12:2).

"But seek ye first the kingdom of God, and his righteousness; and all these things shall be added unto you" (Matthew 6:33).

"Now the God of hope fill you with all joy and peace in believing, that ye may abound in hope, through the power of the Holy Ghost" (Romans 15:13).

This world wants to lure you, distract you, and rob you of your abundant life. We may not want to admit or recognize our weaknesses, but to live in this world and not have them is unrealistic.

Perhaps our weakness is socially acceptable, but is it spiritually acceptable? Is the Spirit of the Lord that is within you telling you that you are selling yourself short? Is the Spirit of the Lord telling you that God has a better happiness for you, but you are distracting yourself from it?

Even if you struggle with drugs, alcohol, a twisted relationship, violence, shopping, eating, social media, video games, exercise, hobbies, sports, or work, you are just as fabulous and amazing as anyone else in this world. Or maybe I should say that everyone else in the world is just as filthy and wretched as you, and that is why we need a Savior. It is only through Jesus Christ that we are fabulous and amazing and—most of all—forgiven. It is only through him that we can find the abundant life God has prepared for us.

Perhaps your addiction is not socially acceptable and is concealed and burdens you with shame. I tell you praise God and worship the Lord with a loud voice and with pride and without shame. Let your heart be filled with the love God has for you. God knows what you are made of. He made you. He knows his purpose for you. He has plans for you too.

As Christians who are forgiven of our trespasses, we have to forgive others of theirs. Addictions are terrible, and they destroy lives—not just the lives of the addicted but the lives of their loved ones as well. It's sad to watch people you love miss out on the wonderful things God has to offer them. It's scary to watch, knowing they may ultimately die from the addiction. Our addictions isolate us. They box us in, and the longer we submit to the addiction, the harder it becomes to escape.

Society, family, or friends don't make it any easier because the shame is so heavy and burdensome it's hard to face them. It's hard to go to them with the truth. I hope that will change one day. I hope the day will come when the world can handle it, when there is no social class for any addiction, and when we can openly face the truth and help each other fight for the abundant life Jesus came to give.

"The thief cometh not, but for to steal, and to kill, and to destroy: I am come that they might have life, and that they might have [it] more abundantly" (John 10:10).

Meanwhile, all I can tell you is that God *can* handle it. God is truth. He knows all and can end all. The shame doesn't exist with God. He has empathy. Why? Because he made himself a man, was tempted in *every* way. You can trust in him to know what it is you are going through, to understand the how and the why, and to deliver you, no matter how long it takes. Listen to the Spirit of the Lord that is in you. Trust in the love that God has for you.

If you are struggling with any addiction—any lust of this world, anything to which you feel bound—have hope. Have peace. Relieve yourself of the shame and guilt that Satan wants you to feel. Rest in knowing that Jesus Christ conquered death and sin … for you.

Addictions are the snare of Satan. He wants us to be isolated and boxed in by our own shame and embarrassment. He does not want God to be able to bless us with the good things in life; so he uses the lusts of this world to occupy our time. He will use any addiction or desire he can to distract us and keep us busy. In doing so, we are bound by guilt, shame, and sadness. Living a life in grief. Missing out.

This is where the battle lies. It's not about what you are addicted to or why. It's about fighting the good fight to defeat Satan's tricks and to give God all the glory. It's about relying on God to help you cope during the bad times. Make God your coping mechanism, and give him the glory. It's about putting your hope and faith in God.

We all are struggling—not just a few drug addicts—and we all need to be fighting together, without labels or categories and without one versus another. The more divided and judgmental we are about the many addictions of the world, the more power we are giving to Satan to continue on his quest of destroying lives.

Saying one addiction is worse than the other is the best way to help Satan to conquer and divide the people—to hurt and isolate them, to destroy each other, and to turn them against each other. To say "God loves you, and there is nothing anyone can do about it" is a slap to Satan's face. Take back the abundant life God has for you, even if you may be the most lured and distracted.

It's time for us to unite in Christ through the power of the Holy Spirit. It's time to support and love one another. All addictions are bad; there are no categories. All addictions rob you of your abundant life, but never let it rob you of God's love.

> Blessed [is] the man that endureth temptation: for when he is tried, he shall receive the crown of life, which the Lord hath promised to them that love him. Let no man say when he is tempted, I am tempted of God: for God cannot be tempted with evil, neither tempteth he any man: But every man is tempted, when he is drawn away of his own lust, and enticed. Then when lust hath conceived, it bringeth forth sin: and sin, when it is finished, bringeth forth death. (James 1:12–15)

Every human is tempted. Our lives on earth are in a constant battle between good and evil, the flesh and the spirit. No one wins. We all fall short. Who, then, can point a finger or shame another? No one. We must support each other and love each other. Communicate openly, lovingly, and with empathy and compassion. God would have it no other way. He is refuge and freedom. We should live in his way, be like him, love like him, and treat others the way he would treat them—with open arms.

"But the God of all grace, who hath called us unto his eternal glory by Christ Jesus, after that ye have suffered a while, make you perfect, stablish, strengthen, settle [you]" (1 Peter 5:10).

"If the Son therefore shall make you free, ye shall be free indeed" (John 8:36).

"And call upon me in the day of trouble: I will deliver thee, and thou shalt glorify me" (Psalm 50:15).

"Submit yourselves therefore to God. Resist the devil, and he will flee from you" (James 4:7).

My message to you is this: don't let *anyone* in the world judge you for your addiction (including me). As I've mentioned, we all struggle with addictions of different sorts and different magnitudes. God, however, has no limitations on his love; he has no boundaries for his grace and his ability to free you.

I often hear, "Turn from your wicked ways and go to God," or "Change your evil ways and turn to God," or "Quit living in your sins and come to God."

This sounds good from the pulpit or shouted from the street corner, but it's not effective. In my time of need, when I was condemned for my actions and was emotionally and mentally lost, I wasn't able to turn from my wicked ways. I had lost confidence in my own strength. I had given up on my abilities to do anything good for myself. I was hopeless. How was I to fix everything and then go to God? I wasn't ever able to do that. That, my friends, is an unrealistic expectation, a false hope, and a pointless and silly phrase. You cannot defeat your problems. You wouldn't have problems if that were the case because the you inside doesn't want these problems. The problems want you, and you aren't capable of defeating them.

What we should be shouting is, "Turn to God, and he will free you from your problems." "Pray to God and cling to God, and he will help you." Put God first and problems second. You do not need to get out of a situation so that you can come to God. *No!* Come to God to get out of a situation. Come to God so you can cope with a situation.

If you are looking to be set free of something, remember that this stuff doesn't happen overnight. I have seen God make crazy changes in an instant, but mostly it takes a while. Pray and be patient. Be committed, and don't give up believing that God can turn things around because he *will*. Don't think you can turn things around. Come as you are, with all your baggage. Feel God's love for you, and welcome God into your life to take control and make the changes he sees fit. Have faith, not shame.

God will defeat. God will win. You can give him thanks for that. Even when you are in the addiction, give God thanks for the freedom you know will come someday. Praise him and thank him for his love for you.

LGBT

10

LGBT stands for lesbian, gay, bisexual, and transgender. I did a Google search of "LGBT and religion" and got the following results. Read through them, and think about what you are reading.

- "The Religious Right's hostility toward LGBT Americans is well known. For years, fundamentalist religious-political organizations have spewed hateful venom."
- "Religion has been a source of both solace and suffering for many lesbian, gay, bisexual, transgender, and queer Americans."
- "Christian denominations have a variety of beliefs about LGBT people, and the moral status of same-sex sexual practices and gender variance. LGBT people may be barred from membership, accepted as laity, or ordained as clergy, depending on the denomination."
- "Religion has not always been kind to the LGBT community."
- "There is a direct correlation to the anti-LGBT theology shared by religious leaders to the violence to LGBT people."
- "The number of homeless LGBT teens—many cast out by their religious families—quietly keeps growing."

Let me highlight the following: Hostility. Hateful. Suffering. Barred. Variety of beliefs. Not always kind. Violence. Homeless. Cast out.

In our society today, these words are commonly associated with religion and the LGBT community. How is this possible, especially with Christianity?

A Christian is someone who believes that Jesus is the Christ and the Son of God, who believes the scriptures in the Bible and that God is our Creator and is love. How, then, could Christianity be associated with these words in any way? Could these same words be used to describe Christ?

Let me try it: Jesus Christ was hostile and hateful, offered suffering, and barred people from his life. He had a variety of beliefs and was not always kind. He was violent and cast people out of their homes to be left homeless.

Does this sound like the Jesus you've heard about? It sure doesn't sound like the Jesus I was raised to know. It doesn't sound like the Jesus I learned about in Sunday school. It doesn't sound like the Jesus I have read about and loved all these years. So what is going on? Why are so-called religious people being hateful, violent, or hostile?

I find myself confused and often shaking my head because hatred and violence is *not God*.

"For the earth is filled with violence through them; and, behold, I will destroy them with the earth" (Genesis 6:13).

"The Lord trieth the righteous: but the wicked and him that loveth violence his soul hateth." (Psalms 11:5)

"Wherefore, my beloved brethren, let every man be swift to hear, slow to speak, slow to wrath: For the wrath of man worketh not the righteousness of God" (James 1:19-20)

Violence is clearly not what God promotes.

I think it is important that we all agree that hostility, hatred, and violence are not acceptable behaviors in association with Christianity. Hostility, hatred, and violence are not, under any circumstance, an accurate display of God's will and love. Hostility, hatred, and violence are not an accurate representation of the Lord and Savior, Jesus Christ.

From where do these conflicts evolve?

"Thou shalt not lie with mankind, as with womankind: it is abomination" (Leviticus 18:22).

That is what it says in Leviticus. No one can contest this verse is in the Bible. It also says:

"For this cause God gave them up unto vile affections: for even their women did change the natural use into which is against nature: And likewise also the men, leaving the natural use of the woman, burned in their lust one toward another, men with men working that which is unseemly, and receiving in themselves that recompence of their error which was meet." (Romans 1:26-27)

Taken at face value, these verses can be direct and hurtful. They could also lead someone to believe that God does not love those to which it refers. That is why it is so important to read and understand the entire Bible. Because God DOES love those to which it refers. As a matter of fact "God so loved the world that he gave his only begotten Son, that whosoever believeth in him should not perish, but have everlasting life." (John 3:16)

In order to drive that point home even further, let's take a look at how these verses fit into the whole story.

Let's start with the Book of Leviticus. The Book of Leviticus is located in the Old Testament (before Christ) and was God's laws for the twelve tribes of Isreal. These laws were given to the high priest of Isreal (the Levites) to then be given to God's people (the twelve tribes of Isreal). Very similar to the laws we have in today's society, these laws were designed to protect them and keep peace; however the laws were derived from the Lord God rather than government.

The lists of laws is very long. Some of them are common, and some are shocking by today's standards. These laws are listed in several chapters, but it seems that the one that is highlighted in today's society is Leviticus 18:22.

Let's look at a few of the other laws listed.

"And if ye offer a sacrifice of peace offerings unto the LORD, ye shall offer it at your own will. It shall be eaten the same day ye offer it, and on the morrow: and if ought remain until the third day, it shall be burnt in the fire. And if it be eaten at all on the third day, it is abominable; it shall not be accepted" (Leviticus 19:5–7).

"Again, thou shalt say to the children of Israel, Whosoever he be of the children of Israel, or of the strangers that sojourn in Israel, that giveth any of his seed unto Molech; he shall surely be put to death: the people of the land shall stone him with stones" (Leviticus 20:2).

"For every one that curseth his father or his mother shall be surely put to death: he hath cursed his father or his mother; his blood shall be upon him" (Leviticus 20:9).

"If a man also lie with mankind, as he lieth with a woman, both of them have committed an abomination: they shall surely be put to death; their blood shall be upon them" (Leviticus 20:13).

"Ye shall not eat any thing with the blood: neither shall ye use enchantment, nor observe times. Ye shall not round the corners of your heads, neither shalt thou mar the corners of thy beard. Ye shall not make any cuttings in your flesh for the dead, nor print any marks upon you: I am the LORD" (Leviticus 19:26–28).

As you read these laws, I am sure you are realizing that they seem a little odd. Keep in mind they were written for a specific group of people – the twelve tribes of Isreal - and they were written before Jesus was ever born.

I'm a country girl at heart, and I like my steak rare. Yet Leviticus 19:26 clearly says not to eat anything with blood. Should I be put to death?

I'm not certain which hairstyle God is referencing with not rounding the corners of your heads or marring the corners of your beard, but for that time and moment, I know he had good reason.

The many laws that are listed in the Book of Leviticus are the laws that are later referred to in the Book of Romans, which is in the New Testament. The Book of Romans was written by the Apostle Paul after Jesus had been crucified and teaches us about what some call "the dispensation of Grace" or "salvation" or "the gospel of Jesus Christ". Whatever you want to call it - It lays out a clear cut message. *We all need Jesus.*

Right in the beginning of the Book of Romans, Paul declares

"For I am not ashamed of the gospel of Christ: for it is the power of God unto salvation to everyone that believeth; to the Jew first, and also to the Greek. For therein is the righteousness of God revealed from faith to faith: as it is written, the just shall live by faith." (Romans 1:16-17)

Paul says about the Gospel – for therein is the righteousness of God revealed. Basically saying, the only way to know what is righteous is to know what is unrighteous, and it is then we truly realize that we are all incapable of ever achieving righteousness on our own.

This is where that second verse fits into the story. Remember Romans 1:26-27? "For this cause God gave them up unto vile affections: for even their women did change the natural use into which is against nature: And likewise also the men, leaving the natural use of the woman, burned in their lust one toward another, men with men working that which is unseemly, and receiving in themselves that recompence of their error which was meet."

This verse is just 2 lines out of 92 lines. Romans chapters 1, 2, and 3 bundle up all kinds of life choices that are exposed under the laws of Moses. It is very easy to pick out these 2 verses and then pick on those they refer to; but what about the other 90? If you read all 92, you will realize that God is *picking* on everyone. He is purposely picking on all of us and highlighting our complicated inequities (according to the laws) that we have literally been born into, so that we may say – I have broken the law. I have failed. I have "fallen short of the glory of God".

The key here is not being offended by it. You can't read these chapters and take offense, because God is just showing us how great his love is for us. We can't forget that Satan continues to try to outsmart God and each of us. This whole law bit, and this is sin and that sin, is an evil scheme of the devil to make us resent God and each other.

But the greatest scheme of all time is the dispensation of Grace.

Why do they call it that? The word dispensation means the *exemption* from rule or usual requirement. The word grace means to be *freely* given. So the dispensation of grace is referring to God *freely* giving us full *exemption* of the laws.

Why is it the greatest scheme of all time? You see, Satan never saw it coming. He didn't know God's plan that God would literally forgive every inequity of every man and free us of the law. If he had known that by crucifying Jesus Christ on the cross that day, that God would be freeing us from the law and justifying us through faith alone – he would have never allowed it to happen. That's why we don't read about it until *after* Jesus was crucified.

God loves all of us so much, that it did happen. Now we are all set free of these laws and are not held according to any of them. Instead we hold the righteousness of God. Imagine being seen by God as 100% flawless and completely perfect despite any laws or anything anyone has ever told you. Imagine everyone that you know, including the one's you don't like, being seen by God as 100% flawless and completely perfect despite *any* life choices.

"*Even the righteousness of God,* which is by faith of Jesus Christ unto all and upon all that believe. Being justified freely by his grace through the redemption that is in Christ Jesus." (Romans 3:22-24)

There it is says it. The *righteousness* of God – by *faith* in Jesus – upon *all.*

"Therefore we conclude that a man is justified by faith without the deeds of the law" (Romans 3:28)

There it says it again. *Justified without the deeds of the law.* This means you are accepted and loved without any calculations of what you do and don't do. I know this may seem shocking to many of you. It was shocking to me when I first learned about it, but it *is* the truth. It *is* the gospel. It *is* what the Bible says.

Romans chapter 3:21 starts out "But now..." Everything leading up to that point in Romans is talking about the law and the law was meant to prove that man is incapable of living up to God's laws. But then it gets to Romans 3:21 and it says "But now.." and the love of God just starts pouring out page after page. It is the beginning point for the dispensation of grace. God places us under grace through Christ so we are free from the law. Now the laws have nothing to do with salvation. Nothing. But now...Satan cannot hold us with the law. He cannot separate us from God with the law. His plan has always been to trick us into to *breaking* the laws, so that we would be separated from God, but now that that doesn't work anymore – what can he do? He can trick us by keeping us from ever understanding or learning about God's plan.

Trust me when I tell you that the devil *does not* want you to know that you are no longer held to these laws. He doesn't want you to know about the dispensation of grace, the gospel of Jesus Christ. He wants you to keep judging others so that you might be judged. He wants the world to keep judging you. It's all he has now. He wants the world to believe that to be a Christian is to be judgemental and a hypocrite, so he provokes hatred and violence. He wants the world to believe that God does not love them and that he judges them harshly for their life and everything they *do*.

But it is not the truth. We have to *all* be ready to overcome his schemes and to stand our ground in faith.

There is no room for bragging about our good deeds. There is no place for accusing others. There is no hope in "doing what's right". It is ONLY through faith that we are saved.

I read this verse often in my own life and it encourages me and reminds me that attacks on me are not of people, and that I can overcome them. Knowing that you face many attacks, I encourage you to also cling to these words of encouragement.

"Finally, be strong in the Lord and in His might power. Put on the full armor of God, so that you can make your stand against the devil's schemes. For our struggle is not against flesh and blood, but against the rulers, against the authorities, against the powers of this world's darkness, and against the spiritual forces of evil in the heavenly realms." (Ephesians 10-12)

Remember in times you feel attacked, by your parents, your siblings, your friends, strangers, whoever it may be, that this is just one of Satan's evil schemes and you need to just be strong in the Lord and trust His mighty power. Know the Word of God, because it is your armor and will allow you to make your stand. This passage goes on to say

"Therefore take up the full armor of God, so that when the day of evil comes, you will be able to stand your ground, and having done everything to stand. *Stand firm then*, with the belt of truth fastened around your waist with the breastplate of righteousness arrayed and with your feet fitted *with the readiness of the gospel of peace*. In addition to all this, take up the shield of faith, with which *you can extinguish all the flaming arrows of the evil one*. And take up the helmet of salvation and sword of the Spirit, which is the Word of God". (Ephesians 13-17)

Satan wants to offend you and provoke you. He wants to offend and provoke those around you. How you react matters. Take this passage to heart. Do what it says. *Stand firm. Be ready with the gospel of peace. Your faith can extinguish all the flaming arrows of the evil one.*

We have been focusing on the law and now that we have been set free of the law, the question always arises; "So what now? We just do whatever we want?" The answer is no. God loves us, and in turn we love Him. Therefore we need to obey in love. But obey what? This is where I want to introduce the New Covenant.

> Behold, the days come, saith the LORD, that I will make a new covenant with the house of Israel, and with the house of Judah: Not according to the covenant that I made with their fathers in the day that I took them by the hand to bring them out of the land of Egypt; which my covenant they brake, although I was an husband unto them, saith the LORD: But this shall be the covenant that I will make with the house of Israel; After those days, saith the LORD, I will put my law in their inward parts, and write it in their hearts; and will be their God, and they shall be my people. And they shall teach no more every man his neighbour, and every man his brother, saying, Know the LORD: for they shall all know me, from the least of them unto the greatest of them, saith the LORD: for I will forgive their iniquity, and I will remember their sin no more. (Jeremiah 31:31–34)

We read in Jeremiah that God made a new covenant for Isreal. "Not according to the covenant that I made with their fathers, when I took them by the hand to bring them out of the land of Egypt." He is talking about the covenant or laws we read about in Leviticus. God has made a new covenant.

Then he goes on to say, "I will put my law in their inward parts, and write it in their hearts." The law of God is in your heart. It's not in a book anymore. It's not in a church or held tightly by a pope, priest, or preacher, or your parents. It's in your heart. Why? Because God is your God, and you are one of his people. I'm not making this up; it's in the Bible.

"After those days, saith the LORD, I will put my law in their inward parts, and write it in their hearts; and will be their God, and they shall be my people" (Jeremiah 31:33).

Sometimes we just get hung up on the tangible. A list of dos and don'ts is much easier than following your heart. Listening to the Holy Spirit that lives inside of you might seem unusual, but if it's not true, then why does God go on to say …

"And they shall teach no more every man his neighbor, and every man his brother, saying Know the Lord" (Jeremiah 31:34).

It sounds like God is telling us not to preach to one another anymore. Why would he do that? He tells us why.

"For they shall all know me, from the least of them unto the greatest of them, saith the Lord: for I will forgive their iniquity, and I will remember their sin no more" (Jeremiah 31:34).

This is such a crucial part for those of us who have no formal education in biblical studies. If you have never read the Bible and think you have no credibility because of it, guess what? God is in your heart, and so are his laws. You know (without realizing that you know) that what God has put in your heart has much more credibility than anything anyone can teach you. Have no doubt. Be confident in your relationship with God. You don't need another person to help you in that area. It is all there in your heart. God told us that; it is scripture and cannot be argued. *This is the new covenant.* The only person who can keep you from a relationship with God and prevent the forgiveness and freedom through Jesus Christ is *you*.

Here's the new commandment:

"A new commandment I give unto you, That ye love one another; as I have loved you, that ye also love one another. By this shall all men know that ye are my disciples, if ye have love one to another" (John 13:34–35).

Love one another as God has loved us. What a beautiful order. What an amazing law. Why is that so hard? The one thing God asks of us is that we love one another the way he loves us.

> That at that time ye were without Christ, being aliens from the commonwealth of Israel, and strangers from the covenants of promise, having no hope, and without God in the world: But now in Christ Jesus ye who sometimes were far off are made nigh by the blood of Christ.
>
> For he is our peace, who hath made both one, and hath broken down the middle wall of partition between us; Having abolished in his flesh the enmity, even the law of commandments contained in ordinances; for to make in himself of twain one new man, so making peace; And that he might reconcile both unto God in one body by the cross, having slain the enmity thereby: And came and preached peace to you which were afar off, and to them that were nigh.
>
> For through him we both have access by one Spirit unto the Father. Now therefore ye are no more strangers and foreigners, but fellow citizens with the saints, and of the household of God; And are built upon the foundation of the apostles and prophets, Jesus Christ himself being the chief corner stone. (Ephesians 2:12–20)

Living today, we have it good. Why? Because we have Jesus Christ. Prior to him, we were separated from God, without hope. Jesus brought us "nigh," or near, to God. He is our peace and has brought down the wall that separated us from God. We are one with him in spirit. Jesus abolished the "enmity," or hostility and conflict. He abolished the commandments contained in ordinances. He came and preached peace and "reconciled," or restored, the relationship we have with God when he was sacrificed and died on the cross. Because of that, Jesus is our cornerstone. He is our connection to God, and we are one with them through spirit. We are already one with the "apostles and prophets," "fellow citizens with the saints," and of the "household of God." As you are reading this, think about it. You are already there. What happens here doesn't matter; we are already there. God just asks us to love one another and to listen to our hearts.

> What shall we say then? Shall we continue in sin, that grace may abound? God forbid. How shall we, that are dead to sin, live any longer therein? Know ye not, that so many of us as were baptized into Jesus Christ were baptized into his death? Therefore we are buried with him by baptism into death: that like as Christ was raised up from the dead by the glory of the Father, even so we also should walk in newness of life. (Romans 6:1–4)

What is there left to say? Let's walk together in the newness of life. The scripture makes it clear that all men are loved by God. The old covenant is gone, and a new one has been made through Jesus Christ. There is only one command now. That we love one another as God has loved us.

"A new commandment I give unto you, That ye love one another; as I have loved you, that ye also love one another. By this shall all men know that ye are my disciples, if ye have love one to another" (John 13:34–35).

REMEMBER NUMBER FIVE

11

There are about 7.5 billion people on the planet. Could you imagine if you could interview all of those people and carefully select your parents? Obviously, you would choose the most amazing people who are perfect in every way and who do nothing but bring positive and wonderful joy to your life. Wouldn't you? Well, good luck with the hunt. It would be a total waste of time and bring disappointment because you and the parents you have were carefully connected by God—a perfect fit for a perfect plan.

The relationship between parents and children is one of the most powerful relationships we ever have. That is why it's a popular topic for people in therapy, prison, rehab, and so on. This relationship between children and their parents influences years and years of emotional, mental, and spiritual decisions. I would even say it plays a large role in marriages and divorces as well. The relationship between a person and his or her parents drives many factors in life.

But what does God say about this powerful relationship?

Most of us are familiar with the Ten Commandments. It's a short list and to the point.

Consider this: if you were God, and you had to come up with only ten commands for the world to live by, what would they be? Put some serious thought into this. Try to come up with ten commandments that would make the world great if everyone obeyed them. Well, this is what God did. He gave us his ten.

And God spake all these words, saying, I am the Lord thy God, which have brought thee out of the land of Egypt, out of the house of bondage.

Thou shalt have no other gods before me.

Thou shalt not make unto thee any graven image, or any likeness of any thing that is in heaven above, or that is in the earth beneath, or that is in the water under the earth.

Thou shalt not bow down thyself to them, nor serve them: for I the Lord thy God am a jealous God, visiting the iniquity of the fathers upon the children unto the third and fourth generation of them that hate me; And shewing mercy unto thousands of them that love me, and keep my commandments.

Thou shalt not take the name of the Lord thy God in vain; for the Lord will not hold him guiltless that taketh his name in vain.

Remember the sabbath day, to keep it holy.

Six days shalt thou labour, and do all thy work:

But the seventh day is the sabbath of the Lord thy God: in it thou shalt not do any work, thou, nor thy son, nor thy daughter, thy manservant, nor thy maidservant, nor thy cattle, nor thy stranger that is within thy gates:

For in six days the Lord made heaven and earth, the sea, and all that in them is, and rested the seventh day: wherefore the Lord blessed the sabbath day, and hallowed it.

Honour thy father and thy mother: that thy days may be long upon the land which the Lord thy God giveth thee.

Thou shalt not kill.

Thou shalt not commit adultery.

Thou shalt not steal.

Thou shalt not bear false witness against thy neighbour.

Thou shalt not covet thy neighbour's house, thou shalt not covet thy neighbour's wife, nor his manservant, nor his maidservant, nor his ox, nor his ass, nor any thing that is thy neighbour's. (Exodus 20:1–17)

In summary:

1. No other gods.
2. Don't make or bow to any graven images.
3. Don't take the Lord's name in vain.
4. Keep the Sabbath holy.
5. Honor your father and mother.
6. Don't kill.
7. Don't commit adultery.
8. Don't steal.
9. Don't lie.
10. Don't covet other people's stuff.

These are what God decided were the best ten rules.

If I were making my list, I would put them in order of importance to me, so I assume God put the Ten Commandments in order of importance to him. If you read them, it makes sense. The first four are all about him. Put him first. Worship him. Don't take his name in vain. Save the Sabbath day for him.

Forty percent of the commandments are all about him. This is in line with everything I've written. Give it all to him. Let him be the reason for the things you do. Give him the glory by relying on him to give you a good life and to protect you and provide for you. It's all about him, not you or anyone else. And again, there's nothing anyone can do about it. He is the ultimate power.

Commandments six through ten are about what *not* to do. These things are no-brainers. And a few would make it on my list—don't kill, cheat, steal, or lie. We can all agree those things never lead to anything peaceful. "Don't covet" makes sense, but I wouldn't have thought of it. Many people never enjoy the blessings God gives them because they measure their lives against the lives of others. They miss out on the maximum joy and peace and what is ultimately best for them. If none of us ever had the influence of other people's possessions, accomplishments, adventures, and all their pictures on social media, we would be able to turn our attention to what we have—the amazing things in our lives that God gave us for a reason. So, I get it. Number ten makes sense too.

Number five, however, is the one that I believe many people would be most likely to leave off the list.

The first thing God listed after discussing our relationship with him was our relationships with our parents. It must be because he knows how important it is and how much it affects our lives. Whether or not you honor your parents can impact whether or not you have a joyous, peaceful, and enjoyable life. We need to rethink how we interact with our parents and what role they play in our lives. As parents, we should rethink how we interact with our children and what role we play in their lives.

The power of the relationship between parents and children and the incredible influence it has is astonishing. It gets overlooked way too much. Often, we only acknowledge it a few times a year—Mother's Day, Father's Day, and your parents' birthdays.

"Honour thy father and thy mother: that thy days may be long upon the land which the LORD thy God giveth thee" (Exodus 20:12).

Let's start with the word *honor*. Why did God choose this word over other words? He didn't say glorify or worship your father and mother; he said honor.

By definition, it means he wants us to regard them with great respect; admire them; look up to them; appreciate, value, and cherish them.

The question is, how hard is it for you to carry out this command? Are you actually doing it? Are you taking it as seriously as the other nine commandments? For some of us, this commandment is the hardest to live by.

Stories are endless with regard to parents, but here is one that inspired this topic for me. I know several people in their twenties who are working hard to become successful in life, to achieve their goals, and to earn the lifestyle they desire. After talking to them, however, it seems that none of those things is their main drive. I've learned their weaknesses, and I've heard their frustrations. I believe their motivating factor and drive is their parents' affirmation and approval; they desperately seek it.

It does work to their advantage because they are becoming successful and working hard to get there. The disappointing thing is that they aren't getting the reward—the joy, the peace, the happiness, the fulfillment. What they are striving for is the unattainable.

Many of us are like this at some point in our lives. We seek affirmation and approval from our parents. Is that what God commanded us to do? To seek approval and affirmation from our fathers and mothers? No.

The commandment says to honor them.

So should our parents praise our every decision and accomplishment and support our life choices? I don't think they're meant to do that at all. As a matter of fact, this is the evil movement in the world, tripping us up and causing us to miss the mark with big number five of the commandments. We are misunderstanding what the relationship between parents and children should look like, not just as children but as parents too. We are missing the mark and probably are being robbed of a lot of joy and healthier, happier family relationships. It may even be affecting the financial futures of our families and estates.

Let's talk about parents. My children are not yet adults, but I dread the day when they'll have to go through life's challenges, failures, and defeats, let alone relationships. I know it will be a struggle for us, but I hope I can follow the simplicity of God's command and not get too wrapped up in it.

As parents we assume an authoritative role because that is our job for our children's first eighteen years. God refers to himself as the Father. God sent Jesus, his Son, to earth to fulfill a plan, designed by God, to save the world. That is a huge responsibility. It's also a huge expectation. Yet God gave Jesus free will. So God allowed Jesus to come here and decide for himself if this was something he actually wanted to do. Jesus grew up, figured it out, and decided on his own that he wanted to fulfill the plan and die to save the world.

As parents or as children, we will never be put into that type of circumstance, but we can learn from it.

God gave his Son free rein, and Jesus accepted the outcome. As parents the only true expectation for our adult children is that they honor us. It doesn't mean we have authority over them. It doesn't mean they are required to take our advice. It means our children should respect and cherish us, admire and appreciate us. (After all, parents are the reason that children are alive and the reason they survive to adulthood.)

I have a two-year-old, and one morning he fell and got a huge gash in his hand. There was blood everywhere, screaming, and crying, all while I was on the potty. Being a parent offers no breaks, no vacations, no excuses. I joke that I am on "suicide watch" at all times with this little guy. So we should be thankful for the time our parents spent to bring us into the world and then to keep us alive.

The responsibility of having children can be overwhelming at times, and it's a responsibility that lasts for years. Staying mentally alert, emotionally balanced, financially stable, and spiritually connected is difficult when raising kids, not to mention that parents are often exhausted. Thinking of yourself first goes out the window, and sacrifice comes blowing in. Yet the love of your child makes everything worth it. When my son started talking, he told me that he loves me. He also added, "You're the best mommy." There isn't a day too long, or a situation too irritating, or a night too restless that can outweigh the value of those words.

I can only imagine how it will feel when he is an adult, and he tells me I did a good job as his mother and that he is thankful, that he cherishes me, and that he respects me for all of my sacrifices. I can only imagine how I will feel when he acknowledges how hard my job was. But what if he doesn't? What if he stops telling me he loves me? What if he stops appreciating me?

To be honest, I never appreciated my parents or understood them as much as I do now that I'm a parent. It has really put things into perspective. I had a fun childhood and parents who loved me very much, but now that I am a mom, I realize how difficult fun can be sometimes. I have a better understanding of discipline and tough love. It likely is the same for most people. Sometimes it's hard to understand and empathize with someone until you have been in the situation yourself.

What about those situations that are difficult? I have already had some moments I'm not so proud of as a mom. I have failed at times. I am not perfect, and my parents weren't perfect, but I know they did the best they could, just as I am giving it my best. If I am okay with being forgiven for my downfalls, then who am I to not forgive my parents for their downfalls?

I would like to take this moment to honor both my mother and my father and their incredible strength, unconditional love, hard work, and honesty, and for being morally sound, God-fearing, and lots and lots of fun. They did all they could to make a good time out of life, with no tolerance for evil. They led by example and taught with understanding and awareness. They were realists and had no problem breaking it all down for us. To this day, I live by their teachings.

Why is it important to honor our mothers and fathers?

Right now, adult children are seeking the approval and affirmation of their parents. "Tell me you like my spouse. Tell me I'm raising my kids right. Tell me I'm smart. Tell me I'm doing a good job at work." Why do adult children want affirmation so badly?

It's a trick of Satan. Satan knows that if we are distracted with the desire for our parents to honor us, we will fail to honor them. This will result in a dysfunctional cycle that will derail God's desire for us, which is an abundant life.

What happens when parents do not feel honored by their children?

Parents of adult children may rebel because they feel they have been taken for granted, overlooked, or disregarded. All the sacrificing and struggles they endured for their children are not recognized. They too seek affirmation, respect, and appreciation. They want to be honored. Without it, they become resentful or closed off, and emotional walls are built. Bitterness sets in. There is an innate expectation in a parent that says, "My child should respect and appreciate me." When that expectation is not met, there is an emotional counteraction.

Perhaps the parents reject their kid's life choices. They don't boast about their children's successes. They may communicate anything but the approval their children seek. They give advice on how things could be better for the child, how other choices could get better results. Regardless, the parental reaction is a negative one.

The reason is because we have the commandment twisted up. Our behavior often is as if the commandment said, "Honor thy sons and thy daughters: that thy days may be long upon the land which the Lord thy God giveth thee."

Is this your expectation of your parents? Is this your kid's expectation of you?

God knows what is best for us. He knows that if we follow this simple command, we will get what we need to live a happy, full life. I even think it goes further into the financial well-being of a family estate. The future generations are impacted without our realizing it.

Historically, land and wealth were passed down through generations. An adult child built his wealth upon the founded wealth of previous generations. Families built establishments that also were passed down to the next generations. We can't say that today. Now, when a young couple gets married, they begin their life together with whatever they receive as gifts for their wedding. Inheritance, family estates, a family establishment—these are all things of the past. Why? Because the family's financial strength and future has been severely impacted by the family's ability to uphold the fifth commandment. Let's look at the verse.

"Honour thy father and thy mother: that thy days may be long upon the land which the LORD thy God giveth thee" (Exodus 20:12).

That thy days may be long upon the land which the Lord thy God giveth thee. I used to believe this was about living a long time. If not for my financial experience, I might not have come to this new revelation, but in sitting with many retirees, I have noticed a common trend. "We don't want to leave anything to our kids," they say. "We are not concerned about leaving anything behind." "I don't want to be a burden on my children." I hear these words over and over, and I think, *Why wouldn't you want your children to have a better financial platform for their lives and their children's lives? Why can't you rely on your children to help you if you are sick or dying?*

Those people have never felt honored by their children. They have not felt respected, cherished, and appreciated by the people for whom they sacrificed and suffered. And now they are bitter, and their hearts have hardened. The end result does have a financial impact, and that is what God is telling us when he says, "so that thy days may be long upon the land which the Lord thy God giveth thee."

Let's say we let go of all our resentment for what our parents didn't do for us—no more *They should have ...* or *I would have had a better chance if only ...* Remember God knows best. He wants what is best for us. So let's honor our fathers and our mothers.

All we have to do is give them the approval, affirmation, and appreciation for our upbringing. That's all. They do deserve some credit for raising us. Am I suggesting we tithe our pay to them, mow their yards, or put their needs before ours? No. Just honor them.

Let's start honoring our parents. Tell them we appreciate all they did for us, whether a lot or a little. Let them know we realize it was hard and that they had to make sacrifices. Say we know they did their best and that whatever they did was all we ever needed. Tell them we forgive them for the bad times and appreciate and value the good times. Let's say we are thankful that they and God gave us life.

Believe that. Cling to it. Acknowledge it to others when the opportunity arises. Let others know that you respect and appreciate your parents. God gave two people out of several billion to call your parents. It wasn't random. He knew what you needed, and he supplied that need through them. Be thankful. Love them as God has loved you.

Ridiculing, chastising, and bad-mouthing our parents goes against the Ten Commandments. God has given us guidance, and if we follow his guidance, we will avoid many frustrations in life. More important, we will have an abundant life.

By honoring our parents, they will drop their defenses. By giving them affirmation that we are not dissatisfied, that we are grateful, that we approve of and respect their choices all those years, we allow them to let go of their fears—fears that we don't appreciate them, that we don't recognize how much they went without, or why they had to do what they did. They can let go of the guilt that haunts them for the times they failed us, for the days when they lost their composure or showed their anger, for the times they abandoned us. If we let go, they can let go too. God says that as children, we are the ones to honor them. It is our commandment to follow.

I have no idea what the outcome would be if I didn't honor my parents. All I know is that it is there among the other commandments as something that's crucial in life. I believe God knows what is best for me and has my best interest in mind. Trusting him has never let me down.

I know what it resonates in my heart. I'm going to honor my parents and hold myself accountable to it, just as much as I'm accountable if I steal, lie, cheat, kill, or stop going to church on Sundays. I'm going to make it important in my life. I more than likely will fail at times, but at least I am going to try. For us to have the life God has in store for us, we all have to try.

As parents, we have to expect honor from our children. Nothing more. Being a parent does not make us kings or queens. It comes with great reward and should always come with honor. God will do anything if you give him the glory. That's all he wants from us. Parents are in his likeness. They will do anything for their children, just to have the glory. It's the way God designed them.

Here's something else worth noting. Every person has two

parents, regardless of whether the mother and father are present in the person's life. There are two people that God has commanded you to honor. Don't get confused about that. Other people are not responsible for your existence. Stepparents, in-laws, a friend's mom and dad—these are not listed in commandment number five.

If someone has been a wonderful part of your life and stepped in to help raise you, you have the choice to respect them, appreciate them, and love them however you want. That's going to happen in all sorts of ways, and you should honor those people. But that's easy to do. Honoring a father who was never around, honoring a mother who chose drugs over you or a father who chose another family over you, or honoring a mother who loved her boyfriends more than you— that's hard. That's where this commandment comes tapping you on the shoulder. And you might think, *That's not my dad. That's not my mom.* Yes, they are. God made it so. You can take it up with him when you get to heaven, but for your own sake, for your commitment to obeying God, and because you have been forgiven, you should forgive your parents, so that your days will be long.

The reason doesn't matter. It might be that you're thankful your dad did the right thing by leaving, so your mom could raise you and not be abused by him. It might be that you're thankful your mom left, so you could grow up without the influence of a drunk. Whatever the story is, find thankfulness. Find respect. Find honor somehow. Search for the good in your parents, and then honor them.

Out of billions of people, you must deal with only two. That's great news if you ask me. God bless my in-laws, but I still have only one father and one mother. They are my husband's parents, not mine. The same goes for my mom and dad. My hubby is not commanded to honor them. The moment I realized that, the better my marriage became. I no longer held him accountable to going out of his way to get affirmation from *my* parents. God doesn't expect him to honor them, so why should I?

When adult children form romantic relationships, they tend to expect their partners to immediately bond with their parents and to love and respect their parents as much as they do. They expect their partners to trust their parents as much as they do and to want to spend as much time with their parents as they do. What usually happens is that time and energy you should be spending honoring your own parents is spent on making your in-laws accept you, and vice versa.

The relationship between children and their parents is therapeutic and very important for emotional and spiritual health. We need more time alone with our parents to become childlike and humble. Typically, our parents offer a safe place and level of comfort that the rest of the world can't give us. It's the place where we can be ourselves. We need time to honor our parents, something no one else in the world can do. Parents need that time with their children too. Aging men and women all over the world with grown children suffer from depression and loneliness because they miss their children. If your spouse loves you, then he or she is in love with the *you* your parents raised and advised.

If you're married, respect your spouse's relationship with his or her parents, and don't be distracted from your relationship with your own parents. Honoring your parents is not a one-time deal; it's an ongoing act. To be a good spouse is to support your spouse's ability to obey the fifth commandment.

If you want to make your partner's parents happy, then let them have time with their child. They will love you so much, as long as their child is happy and healthy. They will value you so much if you let them care for their child. Look out for them. Have concern for them. Protect them. They will value a gift so much more if it is from their child. They will respect your relationship with your partner if you respect their relationship with their child. Would you be an accomplice to a murder or help someone steal a car? I hope not. So don't be an accomplice or a provoker for someone's failing at the fifth commandment.

As the partner, we have to stay outside the boundary of the child/parent relationship that is not our own. If we don't, we may disrupt God's plan and purpose for his fifth commandment. We also might give our time, energy, and honor to parents that are not ours, therefore neglecting the commandment God gave us. Be sure to stay focused on *your* father and *your* mother. Be sure your spouse is doing the same.

Let your parents be your parents and your spouse's parents be your spouse's parents. If you both realize this and respect the fact that your spouse has been commanded by God to honor his or her parents, your marriage will avoid many bumps in the road. Don't keep each other from fulfilling your obligation to honor your parents. Don't provoke each other into talking bad about each other's parents. Don't teach your kids to do that. In doing so, you will rob yourself and your family of God's abundant life for you. If there's an issue with your spouse's parents, it's not your problem, and you should stay out of it.

Be happy that God gave you only two people to honor. When you find yourself concerned about your spouse's parents, take it as a reminder to honor your parents. Redirect that energy and time toward your parents. Don't let Satan trick you.

In remembering God's all-encompassing wisdom and power in our world and beyond, I find it easy to believe that his commands for us are to promote a better life. If we shift our focus from *receiving* affirmation from our parents to *giving* affirmation to our parents, our families will have a healthier, happier relationship, and they will benefit financially for generations to come.

LIGHT OF THE WORLD

12

Have you ever been in a dark room when suddenly someone flips on the light? The unexpected brightness physically hurts your eyes. Have you ever been driving down a dark road when a car comes from the other direction with its high beams on? You can't see the road in front of you because you're blinded by the light.

As a child growing up in church, we always sang "This Little Light of Mine":

> This little light of mine
> I'm going to let it shine
> This little light of mine
> I'm going to let it shine
> Let it shine, let it shine, let it shine

I loved that song. It reminded me that I don't have to be ashamed to love Jesus. I can light up the world with my love for him.

"Let your light so shine before men, that they may see your good works, and glorify your Father which is in heaven" (Matthew 5:16).

Isn't that a beautiful verse? The Bible refers to light a lot. The Word is the light, Jesus is the light, and we should be the light. The idea of light and how light works here on earth is similar to the effect of knowing Jesus and having a relationship with God. Light is a crucial element of life. Imagine life with absolutely no light. Have you ever tried to put on makeup or shave in the dark? Little things become difficult without light. You can survive. You can do many of the same things; it's just not as easy. I'd rather just turn on the lights.

"Thy word is a lamp unto my feet, and a light unto my path" (Psalm 119:105).

As Christians, we turn on the lights by reading God's Word, also known as the Bible. It contains old stories that random people wrote thousands of years ago and that are completely outdated at this point—says someone who has never read it. I always chuckle when my friends say this, because it is so cliché. I've never understood why people just don't admit they've never read the Bible. There's no shame in that. Some try to justify why they haven't read it, as if it's a requirement they've neglected. Just so you know, it is not a requirement. It's okay if you haven't read the Bible.

But for the record, it's *not* just old stories, and it's *not* outdated. Christians use the Word to keep the light on in their lives. Some of us may get busy and not open a Bible for years. Or we never get in the habit of reading it. Still, it's there to help us when we need it. In my experience, it helps. There is so much good advice in there that it will help you to focus on the things that matter and let go of the things that don't. It helps you to find hope in grim situations. It is inspiring and just good therapy.

Life is hard. I don't care who you are, where you were born, what you have or don't have, or who your family is, your life is hard sometimes. But you can flip open a page or open up your Bible app and find out that everything is going to be okay. There is a God who loves you and understands where you are coming from, and he wants to help you. God has more power than you can fathom, and he can change circumstances in a millisecond.

Knowing that certainly brightens my day, and it helps me to press on at times. That's all it is about—those moments when I have absolutely no idea what will happen, and I feel scared and alone and not too sure if I can go on. In those moments, I turn on a little light in front of me. Even though I can't physically see what's in store, I just say, "Forget it. God can see what's up ahead, and I am marching on. So bring it on! I'm with God, and he loves me!" That's what faith is to me; it's trusting in something that I can't physically see because I believe there is another dimension that exists. I only need to have faith that God will have my back.

The Word—the Bible—is there to help you. It will be your flashlight at night. It's there to help you see where to turn or where to take your next step. It's there to brighten your day or your life. It's there to bring good stuff into your life. It's there to enlighten you. If you use it the wrong way, however, it can be like when the lights are flashed on suddenly when you're in a dark room—it hurts your eyes, and you want it to go away.

"For the word of God is quick, and powerful, and sharper than any two edged sword, piercing even to the dividing asunder of soul and spirit, and of the joints and marrow, and is a discerner of the thoughts and intents of the heart" (Hebrews 4:12).

Sometimes people who love Jesus and feel freed from their guilt and pain can get excited and passionate about their experience. They can get so excited and passionate about their faith in and love for God that the light they shine into the world becomes blinding—and others just want to turn it off. Their light is so bright that you can't see what they are trying to illuminate. Still, they usually mean well.

I say *usually* because some people don't mean well. It breaks my heart, but there are people (more than I would like to say) who use the Word of God to abuse others. They use it to bring people down and to highlight others' flaws and misfortunes. They use the light that God gave us to light our paths and be a lamp to our feet in a way that actually turns people away. Rather than lead them forward and help them push on in faith, they use the light to turn people back toward the dark.

Maybe it's unknowingly; maybe it's intentionally. Maybe it's because they haven't truly accepted the grace and mercy that God has offered through the sacrifice of Jesus. Jesus's being crucified to pay for our sins isn't enough for some people. They can't believe that all of their sins are forgiven. The Old Testament is full of laws, and if you break those laws, you will suffer great consequences—at least that was true when the Old Testament was written. But that was before Jesus. That was before grace and mercy was offered to us through Jesus and his death. So those laws are in the Bible, but so is Jesus. Don't let anyone cut you down with God's words from the Bible. That's not what God had in mind. God's words are for good, not evil. Anyone's words (including God's), however, can be twisted to do harm. Remember that God loves you. There's nothing anyone can do about it.

Let's say you ask me if I've read the weather report because you plan to go to the beach. I tell you the forecast is for rain. Now you've been advised that the weather isn't right for a trip to the beach. You've made a decision that matters to you based on my reading and reporting of the weather forecast. Had you read it for yourself, you would have seen that rain is forecast for tomorrow; today will be sunny and beautiful. I didn't give you all the information; I just gave you a small clip. I should have given you the entire forecast. Maybe I thought you were only concerned about the weekend report. Or maybe I didn't read the entire forecast. Maybe I didn't understand it. Either way, you could have enjoyed a beautiful day on the beach, but instead you stayed home. It's important to know that if you want to make a decision for yourself, you should get all the information yourself.

My dad is a coon hunter. I grew up following him around the woods at night. I don't remember ever carrying my own light. That doesn't surprise me. I preferred to have my dad carry the light, and I just followed him. Still, have you ever tried to follow a man through the woods in the dark when he has a light and you don't? First of all, you better keep up, or you won't be able to see where to step. If he gets too far ahead of you, it's just a matter of time before you trip and fall. If you stay too closely behind him, however, you get smacked in the face with the branches he is pushing out of the way. Knowing how much distance needs to be between you and the guy with the light is an art form. Lesson: if you ever have to walk through the woods in the dark, carry your own light.

The same needs to be said about the Word of God, also referred to as the light. If you need wisdom, guidance, encouragement, or to shine a little light on where to go from here, pop open the Book or a Bible app, or visit a Bible website and start reading. (If you can't read, get it on audio.) Either way, you will be holding your own flashlight, and you won't trip or get smacked in the face by someone else's branches or miss out because of someone else's report.

What if you already have a light in your hand? If you are a Christian, a believer, and you have memorized Bible verses, and you are so proud of how much you know, you may think you are armed with the Word of God and that you have the light shining bright for the world to see. You want everyone to know you are a faithful servant of the Lord, and you will pray for others and ask God to help them. If they want to know God, they should come to you because you can teach them; they should listen to you because you know. You are willing and ready to show them God's Word and share scriptures with them. You even may have a Bible to give. If you are out there in the world, ready to flash your light, I am with you. Just remember to keep that light out of people's eyes.

We have to be living in the light for the world to see. The song I sang when I was a little girl, "This Little Light of Mine," reminded me not to be ashamed of my love for Jesus. We have to keep letting our lights shine. We have to let people know that they can come to us, learn about Jesus, and hear from us that God loves them—no matter what.

That means, however, that God has given us a huge responsibility. And just as he did with his Son, Jesus, he has given us free will here on earth. He has trusted that we will respect his plan and his will and that we will not misuse the tools he has provided for us.

When you start talking about scripture, you are picking up a sword. When you pick up a Bible, you are picking up a sword. With that sword you are to protect the weak, the lost, the misled, and the desperate. You are not to use the sword against them, to cut them down, to slice and dice their self-worth, or to bring out their flaws and highlight their wrongdoings.

You are to use the sword to draw them near, to embrace them like a guard who is there to protect them from the evil that follows them and scares them. You are to use the sword to show them they need not be afraid, for God loves them. When they are around you, they should find peace, acceptance, and comfort. That's when they should feel safe. They also should feel set free and loved and so much at peace that they never want to leave your side; you are carrying a sword that can protect you both.

Not only are you carrying a sword, but you also are holding a light for all the world to see. Should that light be bright? Yes! Like a lighthouse! You can see the beacon from a lighthouse from miles and miles away. If you just keep aiming for the beam, you will come safely home.

You should be that bright and that visible from miles away. If you have never taken a tour of a lighthouse, I highly recommend it. It's a long climb to the top, but the view is amazing. It's like God opens the world to you. You can see for miles and miles. Up close as well as from far away, a lighthouse is amazing. But if you were close to the light when it was turned on, you would damage your vision. There's no way you could look at it directly. It would no longer be an amazing beacon; it would be blinding, which is the opposite of its purpose.

The light is a beautiful thing when used correctly. It is an incredible beacon in the night when you need it. God's Word is the same—a beautiful beacon in the night when we need it. It shouldn't be abused or misused. If shined in the eyes of those seeking refuge, they would quickly turn away and flee to dark.

Imagine you were in that dark room, but instead of turning on a bright light, you light a candle. The light would be easy and pleasant to look at. It would bring just enough light into the room to offer a beautiful glow—a small ray of hope, perhaps—and as your eyes adjust, you grow used to the soft light and dependent on it, and you become less comfortable in the dark. It's only then that you could face the full brightness of the light in the room. And when it does get turned on, it doesn't hurt your eyes.

As Christians, we have to be careful not to scare people away or overwhelm them with our passion for God. We have to use God's Word as we're planting small seeds, lighting small candles, being a beacon from far away. We can't walk around shoving a spotlight in people's faces. We have to use the light to guide people out of the dark. Don't allow your light to ever drive someone back into the dark.

One more thing: we have to be careful not to turn the light on ourselves. Sometimes we become so connected to God that we think we actually hold the power, rather than him. Always give God the glory.

Let's say my prayer for my friend has been answered. I should never say, "I was praying for that." *I* didn't answer the prayer. Prayer is powerful, but God should get the glory. A better response would be "Praise God! Thank you, Jesus! God loves you." Then in private, I could thank God for answering my prayers.

If, every time someone gets blessed, I lay claim to my praying, a person could get the impression that the only way to have a prayer answered is through certain people. This, of course, isn't true. God loves you and hears your prayers just as much as anyone's. Don't get me wrong; the more the merrier when it comes to praying. As Christians, though, we can't take credit for what God does. He gets all of the glory. Don't shine the light on yourself and lead people to believe that you have a special connection to God that they don't have. That would be abusing the light and misleading others when it comes to the Word of God.

Keep the light shining outward and not into the eyes of those seeking refuge. Remember that Jesus is the light. Let the light always be on him—not on the leaders of the church, not on your friend who reads the Bible, not on the people preaching on TV, and not on me.

The Spirit of the Lord is in your heart. If the light isn't shining on Jesus, it's not the light you're after.

"Then spake Jesus again unto them, saying, I am the light of the world: he that followeth me shall not walk in darkness, but shall have the light of life" (John 8:12).

WHAT DO I KNOW

I'm not a scholar. I'm not a saint. I have no special ties to God, no special talents or power.

I really had no desire to write a book, but I try to do as God asks of me. I would much rather be writing songs or going surfing. I am happy to be writing this last page. I honestly feel a sense of relief. I am ready for this burden to be lifted and for this book to be finished. That makes me happy.

I don't hold the answers to all the questions. I don't care about debating this verse and that verse. I just want to finish this book and deliver the messages God has put on my heart.

I don't know your problems. I don't know where you come from. I don't even know where I am headed. I'm just a person with issues and flaws and hopes and dreams. I've lived enough and read the Bible enough to know—with all of my heart—that God loves me. I *know* that. I've experienced his love and have trusted it enough times to believe that it's real.

It's not just real for me, though. It's real for everyone. I am no better and deserve no more than anyone else. I know that the love God has for me, he has for you. I know that no one can take that from me. I know no one can take that from you. *You* aren't even capable of stopping the love God has for you. In your darkest times, at your lowest points, God will love you, and he will hear your cry. He is *love*. There is nothing anyone can do to change that. Not even you.

The hate that exists in this world is not of God. People hating people, people judging people, people denying people—that is not God. God is love, and he loves you.

I prayed for God to give me a final verse for this book, and within seconds this one popped up—a final word, not from me but from God to you.

> Nay, in all these things we are more than conquerors through him that loved us. For I am persuaded, that neither death, nor life, nor angels, nor principalities, nor powers, nor things present, nor things to come, Nor height, nor depth, nor any other creature, shall be able to separate us from the love of God, which is in Christ Jesus our Lord. (Romans 8:37–39)

My friends, my family, everyone in the entire world—hear me through and through.

Never forget these words, and never forget that they apply to everyone:

God loves you, and there is nothing anyone can do about it.

Printed in the United States
By Bookmasters